Sura Flow

Sura Flow

3 Steps to Effortless Meditation
& Unexpected Miracles

Sura

ISBN Paperback: 978-0-578-82668-4

ISBN Electronic: 978-0-578-80963-2

Printed in the United States of America.

Sura Center, LLC (Sura Flow)

Sura Kim

suraflow.org

Acknowledgements

To my mother, who first taught me
about energy healing.

To those who feel called to bring peace
and healing into the world.

To my sisters, Chela Rhea Harper & Leah Meyers.

CONTENTS

PREFACE

When I first started meditating, I was in a lot of pain. Back when I was climbing the corporate ladder in New York, I suffered from not only lots of physical pain but also deep emotional pain. Living a fast-paced, high-stress lifestyle took a toll on my health. The lifestyle eventually led me down a dark path of depression.

Meditation brought me back to life. It had such a profound effect on me, all I wanted to do was meditate. However, I wasn't discerning in what technique I practiced and with whom. For years, I stayed at different ashrams and spiritual centers, traveling throughout Asia and North America.

Eventually, I hit a wall. My health suffered, and I was going nowhere. I wasn't progressing — in my life or spiritual path. There was something clearly amiss in my meditation practice. It took me years to discover that what I was missing was a *woman's perspective.*

During my travels and studies, everywhere I went, I noticed a predominant pattern in spiritual practice:

1

male teachers, masculine teachings, and perhaps more notably, male tendencies in meditation practice.

Because of this androcentric focus, there's a misperception in mainstream society about meditation — that it's a difficult practice that requires discipline in order to control the mind.

If you think you have to meditate a certain way, follow the rules, or limit any part of your practice, you may want to consider a more relaxed approach to meditation. If you've ever felt restricted by traditional forms of practice, you may enjoy a more intuitive, feminine approach — one that is open, nurturing, and healing.

In this book, I share my personal experiences and how I came to embrace the creative feminine in meditation practice. This restorative, more surrendered *flow* has transformed my understanding of spiritual practice. It has helped me develop my gifts as a healer — one of the real benefits of meditation practice.

Today we see a predominance of masculine traits in all systems of life, including healthcare, government, business, and politics. We especially see it in religion. It is affecting the health of our world on every level, from climate change to our own homes and workplaces. This is reflected by patriarchal organizations and spiritual practices that are imbalanced.

It is time to move beyond traditional forms of meditation. It is time for us to expand our consciousness to include Her creative feminine energy. Her wisdom, Her power, Her healing magic... Her creative expression. It is the medicine the world needs. Now is the time to evolve meditation beyond its beginnings more than 5,000 years ago. We have different lifestyles today that call for a practice that aligns with our modern lives, for both women and men.

What I am called to present through *Sura Flow* is a balanced approach to meditation, one that is disciplined yet gentle, relaxed yet focused — one that allows us to embrace *both* our masculine and feminine nature fully. A universal, secular approach that anyone can practice. Through balance, we discover more of our true selves. Through balance, we become more whole.

Sura Flow is intended for men and women alike and is inclusive of all backgrounds, ages, religions, and orientations. It simply offers a broader perspective on spiritual practice.

This book contains new ideas on how to complement and enhance your meditation practice so that it is truly uplifting, restorative, and beneficial. When you're truly aligned, you experience a sense of effortless flow. Synchronicities manifest as unexpected miracles. Stress falls away and life takes on an exciting, new dimension.

I hope this guide offers you a clearer perspective and understanding of how you can develop your own meditation practice so you can become more of who you truly are.

May *Sura Flow* bring you a greater sense of peace and wonder. May it encourage you to follow your joy, and may it offer you true liberation.

Love, Sura

INTRODUCTION

Why read this book?

- Learn a softer, effortless practice that cultivates energy, intuition, and creativity.
- Experience Sura Flow™ — a universal, secular practice that helps you develop your life force energy.
- Learn new concepts and acquire new tools that empower you to become more intuitive, emotionally aware, and connected to the mystery of life.
- Embrace both the creative feminine and the focused masculine to help you balance and boost your energy.
- Learn how to "be in the zone" through a relaxed, effortless approach to meditation.
- Develop soft skills and subtle awareness to deepen your practice and enhance your healing abilities.
- Experience greater flow, harmony, and purpose in your everyday life through synchronicity.
- Learn energy tools to gain more energy, slow down your aging process, and feel more healthy and vital.
- Receive practices to help you tap into your human potential and realize your life goals.

PART I

A JOURNEY THROUGH TRADITIONAL PRACTICES

"If you follow the classical pattern,
you are understanding the routine,
the tradition, the shadow —
you are not understanding yourself."
— **Bruce Lee**

CHAPTER 1

MY PERSONAL STORY

A First-time Meditator

When I first started meditating, I was working on Wall Street. In my late twenties, I lived a hard and fast life, which revolved around the stock market — and hedge funds. It seemed I was always living on the edge; everything I did felt urgent, and I was always moving fast. Addicted to the fastness, I was constantly spinning myself into a frenzy. My life revolved around how much I was doing and making, and this eventually drove me into the ground.

Having grown up below welfare in a poor immigrant family, most of my time was spent chasing money and security. I sought the things I thought were supposed to make me happy: a stable job, a romantic relationship, and a lucrative career. But inside, I was growing increasingly empty.

I was vice-president at my company, earning more than I could have ever imagined. Even with plenty of money to buy a 5-star life, I felt hollow. I couldn't bear pretending that the life I had was the one I really wanted. Yet I didn't know *how* to be happy.

My life was falling apart at the seams. I tried to hold it together and keep the happy facade going, but it grew increasingly heavy. Every day I lived in indescribable pain. After a brutal break-up when I discovered my ex-boyfriend had deeply betrayed me, I hit rock bottom. I spiraled into a deep depression.

I resorted to a desperate prayer: "Please, God, please help me find a way to be okay. Help me find a way to *live here.*"

A few months later, I came across a book on Zen meditation at a bookstore. I learned to count my breaths from 10 to 1, over and over. This seemingly simple, yet difficult practice, saved my life.

In Zen, it's said that you should "train as though your hair is on fire." That described exactly how I felt. I fell in love with the practice.

All I could think about was training in meditation. After eight short months, I decided that I would dedicate more of my life to the practice.

Leaving It All for Asia

A year later, I took a leap of faith. I quit my job, rented my New York apartment, and sold all of my belongings. After attending a 200-hour yoga training in Costa Rica, I decided to get a one-way airplane ticket to Asia. I wanted to learn meditation from the source, so I went to India with my backpack.

In the beginning, I had no context for what I was really learning with meditation. I simply did as I was told. But after some time, I noticed a pattern as I traveled through various spiritual centers across Asia.

People often see meditation as an unattainable practice where you give up all your worldly belongings and sit in a perfect lotus pose for hours on a mountaintop.

The biggest pattern I noticed was the rigor and intensity. Many meditation centers followed a structured schedule that was highly disciplined. It was quite strict in some places. There was a silent pressure to sit still in a certain way. When I first learned meditation, I was very rigid. I sat perfectly still but with a lot of tension. I wasn't sure what I was doing most of the time. But I knew I wanted to sit the right way and do the right thing. Inside, I was still very competitive

At that time, people often asked why I was traveling. When I said, "to learn meditation," they all seemed to respond with a mix of awe and admiration, as if what I was doing was an extremely difficult task, like becoming a Navy SEAL. I guess I viewed meditation study that way, too, as something of a major military training! And that's exactly how I approached it. I was very intense about practice and stayed up until all hours of the night studying the ancient texts.

People often see meditation as an unattainable practice where you give up all your worldly belongings and sit in a perfect lotus pose for hours on a mountaintop. This was my initial impression, too, and I was willing to endure any level of pain and hardship in order to learn.

Arriving in India

In 2005, I went to India to learn yogic meditation. When I arrived, I stayed at a yoga ashram in Tiruvannamalai, near Chennai. We woke up before the crack of dawn and practiced on pure concrete outside when it was still dark. The cold crept right into my body, but I couldn't do much about it.

Forty of us sat for hours at a time. Often, it was excruciating sitting cross-legged and perfectly still on cold concrete. The cold dampness crept into my bones, but I didn't dare move or say anything about it.

Every hour of the day was planned. Each day consisted of seven to ten hours of yoga and meditation. This included karma yoga, such as cleaning and conducting duties around the ashram. We had a small break in the afternoon. For the most part, our days were filled with practice from morning until evening, and then it was lights out at 10 p.m. Both men and women wore the same uniforms every day.

The schedule was rigorous. Even more intense were the practices of spiritual purification, like drinking gallons of salt water at one time to flush out toxins. These types of practices not only moved physical toxins, but often triggered deeper feelings and emotional toxins. The more we meditated, the more we purged our past emotional wounds. My old stuff constantly rose to the surface. Sometimes, all I wanted to do was bawl my eyes out. But there was never any time or space to cry, or just be.

This austere, militaristic approach to meditation was something I witnessed in many places. I also watched how this strong approach scared people away. Usually in the middle of the first week, people would break down and cry. It wasn't uncommon to see them pack up and quietly leave. The people at the ashram seemed to know this would happen and would peacefully let them go.

After witnessing this at myriad centers, I began to wonder why spiritual practice had to be so hard. It seemed harsh in the sense that only "hardcore" people endured such intense practices around the clock. Why did we have to learn at such a rigorous pace? Why was every hour of the day so full?

It made me think of the military and how a person's ego is worn down through constant practice and discipline. It shapes them and gets them in order. People who couldn't cut it had to go. However, at the time, I didn't question the ancient system of yogic meditation. It was the reason I had come to India. I just wanted to learn. So, I accepted that it would be hard.

There were days when I wanted to give up. My body hurt. I couldn't move some days. I was absolutely exhausted. I just wanted to curl up like a baby in bed, but I had to keep going, no matter what. There was no time to rest. I would wake up early the next day and do it all over again.

Having come from Wall Street, I was used to doing things at a constant, sometimes unreasonable, pace. I knew how to suppress the need for sleep and rest. That was my MO. I went fast and hard, then burned myself out and totally crashed. So, this type of practice didn't faze me much, until one day something changed.

Unexpected Loss

In India, I practiced yogic meditation religiously every day on my own. I learned the language of Sanskrit with my teacher in India and studied the yoga sutras written by Patanjali. During that time, I lost about 15% of my body weight. I was happy about this initially — I had always been a curvy woman — but after some time, I stopped feeling like myself.

My sense of voluptuousness and sensuality disappeared, and I began to feel dried up and sexless. When I looked in the mirror, I felt more like a man than a woman. The rigorous yogic practice was changing my hormones, along with my sense of femininity.

In yoga, the practice of *brahmacharya* is emphasized. Loosely translated, it's considered "celibacy." I had noticed that separating men from women in spiritual contexts was important so as to avoid sexual desire between the two genders. Women were made to cover our bodies — even arms and legs — when we entered sacred temples. It seemed that sexuality wasn't considered spiritual.

Slowly, I began to distance myself from the idea of being a sexual person, so I shut down my sexuality because it seemed to collide with the idea of being a pure spiritual person. Over time, I began to feel more and more neutered and sterile. My meditation practice was solely from the head and shoulders up. I ignored my own sexual desires. By doing so, I believed I could be "spiritually advanced."

A Loss of Womanhood

After losing weight and practicing so rigidly for so long, I stopped having my period. Every month, at the time when I should have been menstruating, I was in a great deal of pain. I continued to have bad cramps. As much as I didn't like menstruating, I knew it was an important aspect of my health as a woman. It's a vital way to release toxins. I also knew that not having my period was a reflection of having poor health and imbalanced hormones. It wasn't a good sign.

It wasn't until I did a ten-day cleanse fast in Thailand, a year later, that my period returned in full force. It was like hitting a reset button. During that time, I also began to realize that traditional spiritual practices like yogic meditation weren't suited for my body and energy system. They were too fiery and stringent.

That's when *I began to shift my yoga and meditation practice to a softer approach* that felt more feminine and natural.

CHAPTER 2

THE ORIGINS OF
WISDOM TRADITIONS

When I returned to the United States, I contemplated my time in India. As I quietly sat and moved my spine gently back and forth, I suddenly realized a simple yet profound fact: yoga was created millennia ago *by men for men.*

Ashtanga yoga, as prescribed by Patanjali, was not written for women or women's bodies. Practices offered in the yoga sutras are not at all practical for women who are pregnant or on their menstrual cycles (for example, headstands or even *moola bandha,* a practice that involves contracting the perineum).

Between the second and fourth centuries C.E., women weren't allowed to practice yoga, since they were expected to bear children and raise families. Men were the only ones given the privilege to achieve enlightenment. The early practices of yoga came from Brahmins, who were men. They were chosen from India's caste system and were referred to as "men of learning."

Patanjali wrote the first teachings through the yoga sutras. Yoga is an eight-limb system intended to prepare a yogi to sit in meditation for long periods of time. The physical practice of the asanas prepares the body for meditation. The asanas help create suppleness and flexibility in the body, so a practitioner can sustain lotus pose and eventually achieve *samadhi* (divine union). However, this practice was reserved only for men.

The yogic practices were brought to the West primarily by men, such as Swami Sivananda, Paramahansa Yogananda, Bikram Choudury, Pattabhi Jois, and B.K.S. Iyengar. Practices such as power yoga and hot yoga became mainstream in the West but were still very much rooted in masculinity.

Having reflected on the origins of yoga, I had yet another profound realization: ***nearly all world religions and traditional meditation styles were founded and shared by men***. For example, in Christianity, Islam, Judaism, Buddhism and yoga, the central spiritual figure is male. We even call God "Him." All our major religions and practices are androcentric. Because of that, our practices and beliefs are biased toward masculinity.

Nearly all traditional meditation practices — including Buddhist meditation, Transcendental Meditation, and Vipassana — were also founded by men. Mindfulness and other meditation practices are still taught predominantly by men. Spirituality and religion in our world have been almost entirely male-dominated practices.

Nearly every meditation approach has been shared from this androcentric point of view. Consider the effect this has on our spiritual practices today.

This predominant pattern helped explain what I noticed while practicing meditation in Asia and the West. Meditation, in the way it's been taught, has distinctly male energy. It's hard, disciplined, rigorous, and oftentimes militaristic in nature. It emphasizes mental effort.

These types of meditation practices generally engage the mind and emphasize concentration, logic, and reason. It can, at times, even feel forceful and controlling to the point of beratement. For example, at some traditional Buddhist centers, the master will whip a student who falls asleep or becomes behind in his practice. In some retreats, a participant is expected to sit still in a cell from 4 a.m. to 10 p.m. for ten days straight.

*What if we took
a more feminine
approach to
spiritual practices?*

There's a kind of forcefulness I noticed in traditional practices. Many of us have been taught to push rather than encourage ourselves. We're taught to achieve through self-punishment rather than develop ourselves through self-nurturing. These types of beliefs are ingrained in us from the time we are born. They are part of our collective beliefs as humanity, and I believe they are further ingrained through our spiritual practices.

We're taught to self-sacrifice and to self-diminish to lower our ego. We're taught to be quiet. We're taught to keep the peace. We're taught to sublimate our feelings and desires, to believe they are bad and that *we* are bad. We're taught not to trust ourselves but to abide by rules so we can be spiritual.

What if we took a more feminine approach to spiritual practices? What if we took a softer approach, one that is more nurturing and gentle?

CHAPTER 3

THE FEMALE AND MALE PERSPECTIVES

We all have female and male energy. *Yang* (masculine) is considered more dominant and *yin* (feminine) more passive. Feminine energy is soft, creative, and passive while male energy represents power, action, and hardness. These qualities are not limited by gender. Men can exhibit feminine tendencies, just as women can embody masculine attributes.

> *When both yin and yang are present, wholeness emerges.*

Both yin and yang qualities are valuable, but when one is emphasized or valued over another, imbalance occurs. With an imbalance of male energy, a person can become dominant, controlling, and aggressive. When feminine energy is out of balance, a person can become subservient, ungrounded, and flighty.

True inner balance requires both masculine and feminine qualities. When both yin and yang are present, wholeness emerges. Both become potent. In Eastern cultures, the qualities of yin and yang are recognized, such as in Chinese medicine. Notice the qualities that resonate with you in the following list.

Yang energy personality types are often intense, ambitious, and forceful. They may be referred to as Type A. People who associate with yang qualities live in the realm of action, consumption, and achievement. In society, we tend to value this kind of individual who is constantly producing and "doing."

We are often led to believe that being "busy" is a good thing. Today the world is overly yang. We see this in almost every aspect of life, including leadership, healthcare, business, and global politics. It's about winning, dominating, and making transactions happen. Many of us live fast-paced, busy lifestyles that revolve around work, production, and consumption.

Today, in Western culture, we've adopted the Protestant work ethic: "No pain, no gain." It's about sacrifice, constant work, and little reprieve from a yang-based, hyperactive, hyper-stimulated external world. We are all running, racing against one another in a world of speed. Yet few people know what they're running toward. Because of this, people are feeling more anxious and stressed than ever before. Today, anxiety and depression are at an all-time high.

Few of us live slow, quiet lives that exemplify the yin, feminine energy. In the modern perspective, people tend to equate going slow with being lazy or unproductive. When we don't do "enough," we feel guilty. When we take time to rest, we feel bad. We don't want to relax unless we've "earned" it. Yet we need to learn how to slow ourselves down. This is the essence of meditation: slowing down.

Our collective unconscious beliefs related to constant productivity only add to the reluctance to truly let go and do nothing. In a world where constant doing is valued over non-doing, it becomes ever more onerous to be still.

By living in an overly yang-based world, we can keep frantically treading water, or we can make a concerted effort to slow down. More than breaks from using cell phones, we need dedicated time to connect and turn inward. When we don't take time to do so, we may find that our nerves get frayed, we age faster, or worse — we get sick.

Your health benefits tremendously from your ability to relax and slow down. It takes conscious awareness to slow down and be fully present. It takes concerted practice.

Masculine (Fast) vs. Feminine (Slow) Energy

We know that male energy tends to be focused, structured, and linear. Men tend to be more rational and logical, whereas women tend to be more emotional and creative. There are tendencies to the personalities of male (yang) and female (yin) energy. Masculine energy tends to be externally driven, including the search for power, achievement, opportunities, and risks. Feminine energy tends to be more internally oriented. There is a greater need for care, intimacy, and emotional connection that women desire for their own well-being.

Supportive yin energy combined with yang creates true healing for renewal.

Feminine energy has an eye on the whole and relational states of being, whereas the masculine thrives on focus and accomplishment. Yin energy, the female energy, is naturally healing. It provides this medicine through its innate ability to nurture and hold. A child is deeply comforted in the embrace of unconditional love from their parents. Supportive yin energy combined with yang creates true healing for renewal.

When considering yin and yang energy, understand that these values of male and female may be further reinforced through societal conditioning and gender roles. This includes what we've learned is "feminine" and "masculine." However, it's important to be aware of these tendencies so we can better understand how to serve feminine energy through a yin-inclusive practice of meditation. We'll examine these tendencies when exploring today's spiritual practices and how they are influenced by the energy of consciousness.

CHAPTER 4

MASCULINE VS. FEMININE APPROACHES TO MEDITATION

Androcentrism is reflected by world religions and spiritual practices. A key example is the externalization of the divine, for instance, a God that is referred to as a male figure of authority — whether it be a man in the sky, a priest, or a guru.

Designating God as male forms an unconscious bias that men are considered the gender of authority. This bias changes the way we practice and engage in our own spirituality and even in society. If God is constantly projected as a white man in the sky, it imprints a subtle yet profound cultural bias that men represent the "authority."

Positioning this higher, external authority keeps us separated from deeply embracing our own inherent divinity. As a society, we tend to underestimate the power of this suggestion to imprint our collective unconscious into believing, on some level, that male energy is more valuable than feminine energy. The idea of "God as Him" also impacts the kind of relationship we develop with our own sense of divinity.

Meditation is similarly biased, as most popular practices have historically been founded and instructed by men, including:

- Transcendental meditation
- Vipassana meditation
- Metta meditation
- Self-inquiry meditation
- Yogic meditation
- Qigong meditation
- Mindfulness meditation
- Zen meditation
- Taoist meditation
- Sufi meditation
- Christian meditation
- Buddhist meditation
- Tibetan meditation

These practices have allowed us to expand our consciousness, yet it's important to recognize that this masculine bias has a profound effect on our collective understanding of spiritual practice. It affects what we practice and how we practice.

Nearly all religions and cultures acknowledge a "God," a higher power that exists and creates miracles. Take time to meditate and answer the question, "Who is God?" I highly suggest journaling and writing your natural response.

How do you view God? What does God mean to you?

What if God had no gender association? What if God were pure energy consciousness?

When you communicate with God, where do you imagine God is?

There are no right or wrong answers, simply explorations. Our beliefs of spirituality and religion need to be more closely examined because they affect every aspect of life, culture, and society. They shape the way we relate and communicate with Spirit.

Here are some examples of tendencies that represent traditional styles of meditation.

Examples of Masculine-based Tendencies in Meditation Practice

- Mentally focused (mindfulness)
- Strict, disciplined, rigorous
- Hard with strong use of willpower
- Transcend the body and its needs
- Transcend, restrict, or deny pleasure and sexual desire
- Transcend/release personal desire
- Transcend or control emotions and feelings
- Stoic, unemotional, impersonal, austere
- Asceticism, restraint, separation from the material world
- Neutrality, observation, detachment
- Formed, systematic, routine practices/techniques
- External God/authority/teacher
- Less emphasis on healing, imagination, spiritual power, psychic energy, creativity, and applied magic

The bias toward male consciousness results in a more rational approach to meditation — a focus on the mind. Today, many people inaccurately perceive meditation as "a hard practice," one that is about emptying the mind. They assume it takes intense discipline and rigor to control the mind. The idea often scares people away and obscures the accessibility of meditation, which has the potential to be a simple, blissful practice.

At first glance, meditation seems unattainable because it's impossible to empty the mind. But there are other, gentler ways to achieve a meditative mindset. A softer, yin approach gives permission to relax and slip into the state of meditation more easily.

A total surrender to one's true self is akin to melting into the arms of the mother. It is the sweet, nourishing nectar of the feminine that is missing in mentally based meditation practices today. We need gentleness and nurturing. We need positive, loving energy. This allows us to surrender more consciously to the safety of yin, the essence of stillness and receptivity.

The feminine nature of divine motherly love (unconditional love) provides us a strong basis for developing a successful practice. It offers us the security to truly let go, giving us the real support to ascend to higher and deeper levels in our practice. By releasing the grip on discipline and focus, we can allow ourselves to absorb the energy of yin and open further to the bliss of meditation: true joy and peace.

In feeling safe to fully embrace the feminine, one can experience progress in their practice. Yin is the gateway to deeper and higher states of meditation that allow us to truly let go and be present. It is also the basis of true healing. When you are connected to yin, you are also connected to pure healing energy.

Both male and female energies are made stronger when they are given equal value. Effortless action (yang) is received through the feminine energy of non-doing (yin). With a balanced meditation practice, the practice itself becomes effortless. This approach cultivates higher states of being within a practitioner, including balance and groundedness. The real results appear in the quality of one's life outside of meditation, where one can experience greater flow, ease, and synchronicity.

Both male and female energies are made stronger when they are given equal value.

When given the opportunity to tap into and experience the true bliss of meditation, there is no effort or obligation to meditate. Meditation becomes a joyful experience. It transforms from a "practice to endure" to a divine privilege that one looks forward to every day as a way to navigate and thrive skillfully in life.

A Feminine Approach to Meditation

Meditation is more than a mental practice. It's a holistic practice that includes the mental, emotional, physical, energetic, and spiritual selves. What if a meditation practice embraced more of the feminine perspective — energetic and emotional expressions, even creativity?

In many softer practices, the feminine voice and perspective have been marginalized in today's mainstream meditation practices. For example, feminine approaches today are often categorized as "woo-woo," with many forms of healing and magic considered "way out there" or even "crazy."

Yet the majority of people attending yoga and meditation classes are women. They are the majority who have taken a keen interest in developing spiritually, yet even today, many women still learn spiritual practice from men.

Many women are waking up. They are discovering their power. Women are advancing spiritually, but are still often afraid to fully express themselves. This includes their own spiritual perceptions and innermost desires. The reluctance that women experience in sharing their truth often arises from a deep-seated fear they will be judged and attacked, especially in realms that men have largely dominated.

Take, for example, that not so long ago, female healers who practiced healing medicine were persecuted for witchcraft. This trauma still exists deep in women today. Many women are afraid to express their truth and share their natural gifts of healing in public. They don't want to be misunderstood or perceived as "crazy." Today, women are still hesitant to share the full extent of their healing gifts and power. Yet their voices and perspectives are vital to creating balance in our world.

A balanced approach to meditation is what's truly needed — one that encompasses both feminine and masculine qualities. It's time to bring the healing feminine perspective into meditation.

Feminine Expression of Meditation

A woman's touch.

We have often heard this expression. A woman's touch brings energy, femininity, lightness. What if we infused the practice of meditation with a woman's touch?

The creative feminine energy is open, soft, and gentle. In this space, everything is allowed.

There is no control. There is no set way or technique you "have to" practice. Your practice can be anything. It's allowed to go out of bounds. It's limitless. It can even be wild. You can dance, you can sing, or you can throw your arms in the air! It's *all* meditation.

The feminine energy is unconditional. In the space of a mother's love, a practitioner is fully safe to completely surrender and express. There's no one way. All ways are acceptable. There's full permission to take up space. It's okay to fully feel. The feminine approach includes and values the full range of emotions, light and dark. It's all allowed to arise. It's all allowed to be. You don't have to be quiet or stay silent. It's safe to be yourself.

A feminine practice would be more intuitive, purely guided from within. It may also be channeled in a flow state. The purpose of structure is not attachment to the form itself, but to offer a container for emotional depth and healing. With less emphasis on a specific formed technique, it would include the creative realm, a practice created from the present moment. Meditate on what you want, when you want. It is about being in the moment. It's about learning how to be fluid, how to truly live in flow with life.

> *You can dance, you can sing, or you can throw your arms in the air! It's all meditation.*

The creative feminine includes the engagement of imagination, playfulness, and intuitive healing. Feminine energy includes manifestation power.

This energy, whether called magic, miracles, or healing power, is naturally accessible in the realm of creative feminine energy. It's all a natural expression of spiritual practice. Prayer, healing, magic, and contemplation are all one. They are all aspects of one core skill.

The following terms refer to a feminine expression of spiritual practice. It is not limited by gender but describes a general quality of femininity.

Examples of Feminine Energy in Meditation Practice

- Full expression, creativity, chaos
- Embracing, feeling, emotional
- Embodiment, feeling and enjoying the body
- Soft, sensing, sensual
- Receptive, nurturing, sweet, gentle
- Visions, imagination, creativity
- Singing, dancing, ecstatic movement
- Surrender, intuition, inner guidance
- Engagement and practice in the world
- Feeling, heart and emotions are gateways to the divine
- Healing, magic, channeling, prophecy, prayer
- Free-flow/intuitive practices guided from within
- Deep surrender to high vibrations of delight, pleasure, bliss
- God/guidance/authority from within

Perhaps there's a good reason why women, in general, prefer dance and moving with grace. Feminine (yin) movement is flowing, ethereal, even subtle. There's spiritual energy contained in the wisdom of rhythm. More than mental understanding, it's about embodiment, living spirit within the core of your being.

In a feminine practice, there's grace. There's less emphasis on structure, more natural flow. Feminine energy is receptive. You're open to receiving divine energy and insight from the spiritual realm. Through feminine-based practice, you become an open channel, a vessel for light to move through you to provide healing energy to you and those around you. In this way, you become a divine channel.

Feminine energy includes manifestation power.

There is profound opportunity in the level of emotional depth that the feminine has to offer through spiritual practice. Being held in a safe, nurturing, space, like the womb, becomes the medicinal space for restoration and true expression. The feminine energy contains natural healing energy for meditation.

A Balanced Approach to Meditation

When you begin your meditation with relaxation and allow the body to feel safe to release, you naturally begin to open your consciousness to the practice of meditation. We're being called to listen to and honor the divine feminine to further evolve our practice.

In this effortless approach to flow meditation, one can experience profound healing and insight. This is also referred to as "being in the zone" by athletes and artists. It's a state of pure presence. In the zone, you have total clarity in the now. Perhaps you've experienced feeling so connected that you found yourself one with all that is.

In this state of flow, you have access to your higher powers. You could call this your "creative genius" or your higher self. You discover gifts beyond what your ego-mind could accomplish. While being in the zone, you might find yourself graced with extra-sensory abilities (even expanded physical, mental, or psychic abilities).

When you're in the flow, there is often a profound sense of oneness, of connection, of pure existence. There's a feeling of expanding beyond your individual self. In this place, you experience complete unity. It is blissful. This state is deeply nourishing and rejuvenating. You lose track of time.

The gateway to entering this zone is a balance between yin and yang — the feminine and masculine energy. One must be relaxed yet focused and surrendered. To truly go deeper in meditation, it helps us to embrace the feminine energy of softness. When we are soft, we are open. Our energy flows. We are able to receive the nectar of the practice when our hearts are open. Compassion, forgiveness, and gentleness are the pillars of a sustainable practice that truly feeds us. In balancing our yin and yang energy, we become centered and make progress toward realizing our true spiritual potential.

Salt Spring Island

After returning from Asia, I taught meditation and yoga for three years in Los Angeles, where I started my coaching business. I felt called to be there, but it was a stressful time. It took a great deal of energy, and I often felt drained teaching yoga on top of having to drive through massive LA traffic. It wasn't long before I felt burned out. I knew I needed time for retreat.

It was clear I needed to focus and develop my own practice. Even though I had been teaching meditation for several years, I still didn't feel I really "got" meditation. Something about the practice continued to elude me. "What's the point of meditation? What am I supposed to be doing or experiencing?", I wondered.

I wanted to go deeper. I stopped my work in Los Angeles and spent three months meditating continuously in spiritual retreat in the Brazilian countryside.

When I returned from retreat, I was called to go to Vancouver, BC. While I was there, I happened to hear about a place called Salt Spring Island. The moment I heard those three words, I knew I would go there. After a quick Google search on how to get there by boat, I packed up my Prius and booked a one-way ferry ride from Vancouver.

It was the middle of summer. To my surprise, I had arrived at one of the most idyllic places I had ever seen. It was as if I had entered a small force field bubble of peace. I had landed on a pristine island with a small community of artists and farmers. It was full of breathtaking, lush nature, a few stores, and some farmers' markets. It was perfect, and soon it felt like home.

I rented a small, rustic cottage. It had its own private landing on a beautiful glassy lake surrounded by massive fir trees. There was little in the way of modern amenities: no TV, no internet, no phone access or cell service. But it was exactly what I wanted; simple with no distractions.

Since there wasn't a main heating system, I had to take care of my own firewood in the fall and carry gallons of drinking water across a small field into my cabin. It required more work, but it was a retreat experience I had always wanted. My own "Walden." It was a dream come true being in retreat in the middle of nature.

It was there on Salt Spring that I decided to learn meditation all over again from scratch, but this time from nature. I really wanted to understand and develop my practice. Solitude was at first exciting. But as time progressed and loneliness set in, it became unhinging. With nothing to hold onto, I became undone.

All the things I was accustomed to being, in the context of others, lost their shape. Since I was alone, the element of relating to people was completely gone. The usual masks and ego-self I identified with began to erode. With those aspects absent, I got to know myself again but without the roles I was accustomed to: a teacher, a student, a woman of color. Whatever came up for me, I had to deal with on my own. There was nothing to distract me from my own demons. I was there to heal.

Being alone helped me see more clearly the nature of my own thoughts. Without the need to be engaged with others, I could drop into meditation and focus on developing my practice. I took time with everything I did, whether it was hand-washing my clothes or cutting vegetables. In the morning, I'd wake up, make coffee, write for an hour or two, and then meditate for two to three hours before starting the day.

In the warm embrace of nature, I felt safe to completely let go. With more time and space, solitude nourished me. It filled me up in a way I had never felt before. In nature, I experienced deep purification. During my retreat, I moved through many egoic layers, including inner tendencies and patterns that kept me safe but also separate. For example, being strong also meant being independent but not able to be vulnerable and ask for help when I needed it. It was gut-wrenchingly uncomfortable. I vacillated through loneliness, boredom, sadness, guilt, shame, presence, depression, ecstasy, focus, and some crazy. The whole spectrum of emotions arose, some for the first time in my life.

Each layer revealed a part that drew me into myself and into my center. Surrounded by massive, old, green, wise trees, I felt safe to cry. It was as if they were holding me, giving me permission to let go completely. Nature assured me it was okay. Okay to just be. Okay to be exactly what I was. This was a place where I could completely be myself. My emotions, my fears, and everything else I had held back unfurled and were unleashed. The twisted, pent-up, knotted tensions inside began softening and unraveling. It was deeply cathartic, and I found a broader peace.

It was during my time in Salt Spring that the essence of Sura Flow began to emerge, though I didn't realize it at the time. What I needed was to cultivate the lost feminine parts of myself in order to discover my wholeness and deepen my practice. Even years after, I am healing this part of myself.

When I first started meditating, I sat in militaristic fashion. I sat perfectly still and straight, no matter the pain or the discomfort. It wasn't until I was completely alone that I gave myself permission to stretch, take my clothes off, and try new positions. It was liberating to be able to do anything. I swam naked in the lake. This simple act of freedom provided me a new perspective about myself and my body. My body had never felt so good. For the first time in my life, I became completely pain-free.

Every day I laid my body on the earth. It energized every bone. It grounded my sitting practice. It gave me the courage to change and try new things like softening just a little bit. Even in meditation, I held a kind of inner guard, a protection that shielded me. It seemed part of me. It was always there. It wanted to "do it right, be perfect." But with time I realized this guard also separated me from the world, from fully engaging and being with the world. I needed to release this hardness from my own meditation practice.

This subtle but profound layer, hidden within the strength of my persona, began to melt away. It dismantled me. I realized I had been so hard on myself that I used this same approach in my sitting practice. There was a constant forcefulness and judgment consciousness that was restricting me, watching my every move. Silently telling me "the way I *should be* doing it."

This invisible energy inside me didn't allow me to fully relax, trust, and feel safe to be free. I hadn't trusted the softer, finer energies of the feminine because I didn't have a place for feminine energy in my own being. It didn't feel safe to relax or express that part of myself.

It's in the freedom of the practice that we discover the true spirit of meditation: bliss.

For most of my life, I had learned to be mental and expect results. I felt much more comfortable being masculine. With time I was able to feel safe enough to surrender in my practice. I had been going at meditation so long and hard through the vessel of the mind, and I was still tense. I had forgotten about the other parts of my being. My intuitive self, my sensual self, my energy, the wisdom of my body. By nurturing myself and taking action on what I really needed to grow, I developed my energy.

Having a softer practice took away the layers where I hid my deeper inner self. Through energy-flow meditation I had more access to myself, my truth, and my own authentic desires.

The more I deepened into my practice, the more I saw the need for emotional healing, embodiment, and nurturing in meditation. This is how I came to develop a general foundation for Sura Flow. By allowing myself to completely abandon what I thought I knew about meditation, I discovered new freedom and, with that, newfound gifts.

This approach of experimentation and allowance without inhibition is vital for developing oneself. It is the basis for the energy arts; the freedom to flow in any direction that creates balance. In our spiritual practice, we needn't feel restricted because ultimately we are free. It's in the freedom of the practice that we discover the true spirit of meditation: bliss.

Over a period of seven years I maintained retreat in Salt Spring. It's a time that I will always treasure. The nourishing energy of nature helped me understand the value of a softer, energy-based approach to meditation.

.

PART II

DEVELOPING AN ENERGY-BASED
APPROACH TO MEDITATION

*"If you want to find the secrets
of the Universe, think in terms of
energy, frequency and vibration."*
— **Nikola Tesla**

CHAPTER 5

SURA FLOW EIGHT-FOLD PATH

The Sura Flow approach to meditation is creative and feminine. The intention is to provide access to both male and female energy qualities. In balancing your yin and yang, you become centered and progress toward realizing your true spiritual potential. The key to Flow practice is balance.

When you are balanced, you receive divine energy and inspiration. When you connect to yourself through Sura Flow, you can freely tap into your creative energy and expression. We all have chi, and there are essential aspects of ourselves and our lives that affect the quality of chi we experience. This is reflected in the energy wheel below:

Energy Flow Wheel

When these aspects within the self are cultivated, you experience a heightened sense of connection and energy. Your mind creates experiences, sensations, and activates emotions. When it is in balance, you are clear and focused. When the mind is muddied and full of thoughts, you experience a drain on your life force energy. When any one aspect is severely out of balance, you are likely to experience stress, tension, and pain.

The skill in energy-flow practice is to notice the quality of energy in your moment-to-moment. By becoming aware of energy and skilled in your application of chi, you learn how to master your own creative life force energy. You begin to understand the importance of raising your energy (vibration) so you can reach your highest creative and spiritual potential.

Raising your vibration refers to a shift in energy that is clear, present, and grounded. It is a shift in consciousness that you can change at will. When your vibration is low, you are resonating in fear. People who are deeply wounded and unconsciously act out of their wounds resonate at a lower level. By raising your self-awareness and healing through self-love, you raise your energy. When you have a high vibration, you live in a state of peace, calm, and contentment. It is easier to live your true authentic self.

When you experience a low vibration or a leak of energy, it's a sign of imbalance. This could be from having stressful thoughts, a bad job, or suppressing the truth within yourself. It could be a sign of dysfunction, such as being in a toxic or co-dependent relationship where you might experience a rollercoaster of emotions and big energy swings. By becoming aware of your vibration, you can take corrective actions to balance and boost your own energy levels.

When you know what depletes and supports your energy, you can use this information as a guide in your life. A life force that's energized and bolstered is a sign of moving in the right direction. When it is weak and constantly drained, it means that you need to take action to balance your energy. Your life force energy has an intelligence of its own. It is constantly communicating with you. Pay attention to each part of the energy wheel to understand how you're flowing your own energy.

> *A life force that's energized and bolstered is a sign of moving in the right direction.*

Each part of the wheel feeds into your energy system. When you're practicing, it benefits you to develop a clear mind, emotional health, as well as a positive relationship with your body. In cultivating your practice, it's important to be in touch with your own desires and learn how to channel your them through your purpose and passions. Developing yourself through energy leads you to your own sense of integrity and moral compass. This affects the way you live and ultimately your health. When all of these aspects are balanced and flowing, you feel connected to your personal power and purpose.

In Sura Flow, you'll learn how to navigate each aspect to maintain your chi force to maintain a strong sense of health, peace, and balance. When you are free of mental tensions and inner conflicts, you are free to live in harmony with all of life.

Receive Energy From Balance

That "flow" balance is the state between effort and surrender. It's letting the whole body become relaxed while being fully alert. It's a state of presence. *Sura Flow is synonymous with "effortless flow" or Flow practice.*

This effortless approach is simply a guide. It's universal and secular in nature. There is no dogma, doctrine, or beliefs to adopt to practice Sura Flow. You can practice this approach together with any other religious or spiritual path. You may be happy to discover that it enhances your existing spiritual practices, including prayer and contemplation.

You can receive what you need from this approach or disregard any part that doesn't ring true for you. The key is to create a practice that truly resonates with *you*. When you discover a practice you love, you're inspired to do it every day. That means you'll receive more benefit from your hours of practice.

Sura Flow is synonymous with "effortless flow" or Flow practice.

In Sura Flow, there's an emphasis on cultivating the creative feminine energy that lives within each of us. It is a dynamic, vital practice, so you can live fully present in the moment. The creative feminine emerges through deep stillness and surrender. Sura Flow is an approach intended to bring harmony and wholeness to your meditation practice.

Rather than a mental approach to meditation, Sura Flow is an energy-based practice. Effortless flow helps you raise awareness of your own creative life force energy. The more attuned you are to your energy, the more in tune, focused, and inspired you'll be on a daily basis.

This approach is well-suited for people who want to tap into the potential of their creative life force energy. These techniques help you raise your frequency and inspire creativity. There's a focus on imagination, intuition, and listening. Sura Flow is about living wholly in the present moment. When you're tapped into your creative flow, you are tapped into the power of the present moment. You are receptive to the spontaneous nature of spirit.

Effortless flow helps you connect to the energy of the now and to trust your intuition in the moment. In this state, you're clear. No longer burdened by the "shoulds" and "past/future" of the linear ego-mind, you are free to live and express your natural authentic self. The practice helps you release any layers that keep you from being your true self.

The Sura Flow method emphasizes expression over repression, care over control, allowance over force, freedom over restriction, and nurturing together with discipline.

Through discipline, you discover freedom.

The balance between discipline and surrender allows for flow. When you sit every day you create a routine through structure. The discipline of showing up every day empowers you to be receptive to flow energy. When you sit every morning, you show up to the wisdom of your spirit. This bond becomes stronger with each passing day. Continued practice allows you to enter "the zone" where you experience a heightened sense of creativity, connection, and oneness. Through discipline, you discover freedom. Through structure, you learn how to master your energy.

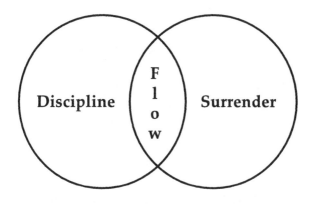

In Sura Flow, you tap into the expansive magic and healing power of the divine feminine. Immersed in this state, your energy can move and rise to its highest level. Through the feminine, you tap into your innate gifts of healing and manifestation. With continued practice of the masculine structure, you become more subtle in your awareness and intuition, entering the realm of pure potentiality. By surrendering, you connect to the true power of healing, prayer, and manifestation. It takes you on a deep dive into the fertile void, the mystery and miracle of life.

Your guide lives within you.

In the subtle realm, you can learn to channel and guide the healing energy of the sacred feminine and access subtle levels of your intuitive guidance. When you learn how to ground this energy together with the sacred masculine, it empowers you to manifest your gifts in the physical realm. Your divinity is inherent. Your guide lives within you. In this space, it is possible to access all your own answers and insights.

Sura Flow is a joyful practice that empowers you to become self-actualized, balanced, and liberated. This softer approach accelerates you toward your highest potential and destiny.

The daily practice of Sura Flow promotes compassion, forgiveness, and stillness. It includes the qualities of the creative feminine energies that support a dynamic, balanced meditation practice.

Sura Flow Qualities:

Nurturing	Intuition	Emotions
Imagination	Delightfulness	Energy
Visualization	Pleasure	Life Force
Softness	Manifestation	Delight
Creativity	Enjoyment	Feelings
Bliss	Passion	Intention
Sensuality	Healing	Prayer
Gentleness	Self-love	Magic
Compassion	Nourishing	Alchemy
Body	Self-care	Visions
Sweetness	Full expression	Power
Ecstasy	Heartfulness	Joy
Sensitivity	Abundance	Flow

When you discover an effective approach that truly resonates with you, you're inspired to meditate daily. You receive the benefit from your practice that includes energy, guidance, and contemplation. As a result of your meditation practice, you may notice an ease and wonderment that unfolds through synchronous experiences.

CHAPTER 6

MIND

*"The soul becomes dyed with the
colour of its thoughts."*
— **Marcus Aurelius**

Many people tend to focus their attention in their mind when they meditate. Their aim becomes controlling or emptying their mind. This can turn into a constant struggle during meditation. The tendency for many practitioners is to focus their attention in the prefrontal cortex, where planning, problem-solving, and past/future thinking happens. Often referred to as the "monkey mind," this is where we spend the bulk of our time, but it's the most difficult area to calm down.

If this has been the way you've meditated, you may have discovered that in trying to focus your mind, your meditation becomes an inner struggle. When you try too hard to control or empty your mind, your practice becomes tense, causing further agitation. You might have experienced sitting the entire time while thinking, wondering if you'd made any progress.

There are other ways to quiet the mind. Consider resting your attention on places within you that easily

55

invite higher awareness — for example, your heart and body. You'll notice that when you focus on other areas, the thinking mind naturally begins to settle down. This is because you're not anchoring your attention and energy in your head, where all the busy thinking happens.

To cultivate a meditative mindset, it helps to recenter your primary focus. Begin with relaxing your physical body and bringing your attention to the center of your heart. It is usually beneficial to close your eyes or have a soft gaze while meditating. Keep the attention in your heart center or the center of your body (the solar plexus area).

PRACTICE:
Centering Your Attention

1. When you meditate, shift your attention from the prefrontal area of your brain into your whole body.
2. Instead of trying to control the mind, take time to relax each part of your body starting with the feet.
3. Practice being energetically centered in your heart and body (such as the center of your heart or your solar plexus).

Why the Mind Matters

Relaxation is beneficial in any practice, even with intense concentration. It helps the mind naturally quiet down. Relaxation slows down the breath and biorhythms of the body. By learning to slow the cadence of your thoughts and witnessing them with a sense of detachment, they become easier to change. Your mind has less of a grip on the way you think. When your mind loses its grip and momentum, there's more space between each thought. Your mind becomes calm and placid. In this state, it becomes possible to experience mental clarity and focus.

When your mind becomes steady and focused, it allows for new awarenesses and intuitive insights to emerge. When your mental state becomes pure, you become receptive to deeper truths. You're no longer caught in a trap of incessant thinking. You have space for new thoughts and awareness to arise. When you are clear, you become attuned to your higher-mind (the superconscious mind that is connected to the essence of the universe). You have access to your deeper wisdom and inner-knowing.

With practice, you'll notice less momentum and more space between each thought. You become empowered to shift your inner dialogue from one that is negative and repetitive to a more neutral mindset. Eventually, you develop the skill to change the nature of your thinking so that you can cultivate positive thoughts. As you progress, you can develop mental strength and power, gaining more mastery over the state of your mind. With higher awareness, you begin to directly experience the creative power of your own thoughts.

Scientists have discovered that we have 60,000 to 90,000 thoughts per day, many of which are negative or fear-based. Some doctors of psychology, such as

Dr. Rick Hanson, have shown that we're actually wired to have stressful thoughts. As humans, we have a "negativity bias" due to our inherent survival instincts. In the past, we had to anticipate the worst-case scenario in order to survive. That means we're hardwired to focus on the negative. This is why negative thoughts "stick like Velcro" much more than positive ones, according to Dr. Hanson, so it's normal to have more negative thoughts!

Healing Affirmations

Observing your thoughts changes their nature. It's also possible to heal your mind through meditation. You can learn how to apply your thoughts in a conducive way by staying conscious of them and practicing positive self-talk. When you do this, you affirm positive energy. For example, you can repeat positive affirmations for experiences you wish to create or embody. You can affirm "I am peace" or "I'm an artist." You can also use your thoughts to affirm your life intentions: "I am realizing my true potential" or "I am aligned."

You will notice that focusing your attention on positive thoughts helps you be more present. It automatically shifts your internal state of being. For example, you will feel a noticeable shift after practicing a 20-minute loving-kindness meditation, that repeats the phrase "May all beings be peaceful." When practiced consistently, an affirmation eventually leaves a subtle imprint in your consciousness. You will feel the benefit of saying a positive affirmation again and again in your own mind.

In this way, affirmations are healing. They become gateways to positive thinking. Affirmations help you release limiting thoughts and beliefs by seeding new positive thoughts that lead to new experiences.

In addition to practicing this, I highly recommend positive self-talk. Too many of us live with constant negative thoughts about others and ourselves. We're silently judging, criticizing, saying things like "good enough"or "not good enough." We think in terms of "good" and "bad." This kind of dualistic thinking often causes us suffering.

> *Affirmations help you release limiting thoughts and beliefs by seeding new positive thoughts that lead to new experiences.*

By becoming more conscious of the thoughts we have *toward* ourselves, we can begin to replace them with positive words of encouragement. Instead of berating ourselves and others, we can take time to pause and recenter. We can start with an observation, such as, "Isn't that interesting?" In this way, we begin to take on a softer, more friendly tone with ourselves.

Eventually, through practice, we can learn to automatically lend ourselves and others the benefit of the doubt: "I did my best," "I'm proud of myself," or "I love myself." When you're practicing meditation, it's essential to cultivate a positive mindset. It's important to actively practice love and compassion toward ourselves.

The Imagination

Albert Einstein said, "Imagination is more important than knowledge." Through visualization and the power of your imagination, anything becomes possible.

The practice of visualization is healing. You can use your mind to envision what you want to experience. Many people have healed themselves of "dis-ease" and pain through the art of visualizing their health. For example, they might imagine a golden light flowing through their body into the afflicted area and change the energy of their pain naturally through the power of their imagination. This is similar to practices like qigong that use intention, visualization, and movement to shift energy.

Artists use their imagination to create art. It becomes the inspiration of their creations. Performers and athletes have long used the practice of visualization to enhance their performance. It's been shown that top athletes benefit from mental rehearsal of their sport by continually envisioning their success. You can create anything in your imagination to bolster your meditation practice. This skill is especially beneficial in the practices of healing and relaxation.

By engaging your imagination, you open up the intuitive facilities of your mind. For example, you may receive a vision of what is to come. You can use your imagination to build your own health and strength. For example, by envisioning a massive tree or mountain. This kind of imagery gives you the power to connect to a resource beyond your individual self. The image of a still lake may help you connect to feelings of deep peace. The skill of imagination and visualization gives you unlimited healing potential and creative abilities.

The practice of visualization is healing.

Shifting Your Thoughts

Through meditation, you realize the power of your thoughts. The universe and people in your universe constantly receive and respond to the energy of your thoughts. It's vital to know the nature of your mind through practice. The more intimate you become with your thought forms and patterns, the more empowered you become to choose them.

Thoughts transmit energy. They shape your life experiences. The way you perceive experiences through your mind affects the way you process them through your body. So, for example, if you view life as stressful and overwhelming, your body will automatically experience stress. The key is to shift your perspective in the way you see and receive your life experiences. Do you generally see yourself as a victim or an adventurer in life?

Your thoughts influence everything, including your face, your body, and your health. Negative or stressful thoughts cause energy depletion and lower your immunity. When you have positive thoughts, they flow through your body and even bolster the health of your cells. According to Chinese medicine, your thoughts and emotions have the power to create health or disease.

Your thoughts affect every moment of every day. They affect your inner life, your outer life, and the people in your life. No matter what, you'll always have thoughts. Why not take some time to slow down and consciously cultivate positive ones? Why not have thoughts that truly support your health, your mental well-being, and your energy?

With consistent practice and observation without judgment, meditation empowers you to consciously be aware of your own thoughts. You get to choose how to focus your mind. By continuously observing your mind with a sense of compassion, you'll experience more space and neutrality with your own thoughts.

Consider the profound ability to be able to change your thoughts at will.

> **Affirmation: I compassionately observe and choose my thoughts.**

CHAPTER 7

BODY

*"Our bodies are our gardens,
our wills are our gardeners."*
— **William Shakespeare**

In yang-based traditions, the body is seen as secondary, a "physical" obstacle to overcome. What's emphasized is the control, denial, and transcendence of the body.

"You are more than the body," we're often told by spiritual teachers. This is true; however, we live in our body. When the body is seen as something to overcome, you may find yourself ignoring the true needs of your body or contorting your body to do things that cause further injury. For example, you can force yourself to sit completely still for hours at a time, regardless of how painful it is. That's how I first learned meditation.

When I started my sitting practice, I was told not to move. I sat and endured pain and numbness for hours on end. While I understood the value in not giving in to distraction, years of this disciplined way of sitting ended up injuring my spine. Now I have a chronic condition in my neck, which doctors have said developed from hours of sitting. Today, I have adjusted my sitting practice by including restorative yoga poses as part of my meditation practice. I wish I had been given options for my sitting practice and had permitted myself to lie down when I was experiencing pain back when I was first learning meditation.

Sura Flow practice emphasizes being present in the body. This means that while you're meditating, you're aware of being in your body (not just in your head). You are inhabiting your whole body, from the bottoms of your feet to the top of your head. When you engage your awareness and connection to your body, you are embodied. When you are anchored in your physical body, you are home. You are connected. This helps you become more clear, present, and focused.

When you listen to the body instead of controlling, denying, or changing it, you can realize the potential of your divine physical instrument. It's true that you are more than the body, but this body is the vehicle through which you create. It is the temple you are given in this life. It's your job to love and take care of it the best way you can through a healthy diet and exercise. In doing so, you'll notice that having a healthy physical body supports your practice and your energy. It also slows down the aging process and cultivates resilience and longevity.

It is possible to be balanced and centered in your body even if it's not perfect. Meditation gives you the compassion and courage to love your body as it is. You have the opportunity to experience it as the miraculous vehicle of creation that it truly is. Through practice, you can learn to be grounded and secure in your body and to trust it as a conduit of spirit.

To develop a sustainable practice, it's important to take care of your body. It's your vehicle for moving through life, which is why it benefits you to cooperate with it. Being present in the body is also a vital aspect of meditation. Today, there are forms of meditation practice that do not address the importance of being present in the physical body. In fact, you may be faced with instructions to control or push your own body. And in some practices, practitioners are encouraged to leave their body as a way to transcend to higher realms of consciousness.

Meditation gives you the compassion and courage to love your body as it is.

Many people leave their body during meditation. Instead of staying present in the physical form, they float somewhere far away in their imagination. There is nothing inherently wrong with this approach; however, consistently practicing this way may cause you to become disassociated, spacey, and ungrounded. You may feel split apart from your body like you're hovering above yourself. As a result of being ungrounded, you can have a hard time creating in the physical world and making real progress in your life.

At the other extreme, people who are highly intellectual may only reside and orient from their head space. When this happens, you have little connection to the rest of your physical body. Even meditation becomes a mental pursuit. With only an intellectual understanding of spirituality, it's easy to get "stuck in the head," living from a place of past/future thinking, logic, and reason — completely disconnected from the spontaneous, fluid nature of spirit.

The body is an important vehicle for raising your self-awareness. It can be a vital part of your path to awakening. What if you loved and honored your body exactly the way it is now? What if you took time to slow down and listen to your body's needs?

The key to an integrative yin-based meditation practice is listening to your body. Your body is consciousness. It doesn't lie; it contains real wisdom. Your intuition often expresses itself through your bodily sensations and feelings. You get that "gut instinct" through your body. That's where you sense your intuition. It's information. Your body is a reflection of your consciousness.

When you have pain, it's your body's way of communicating that something is out of balance. When you are tired, do you rest? Or do you plow through and assert your will against what your body needs?

When we ignore our body's needs, we also ignore the intuition that flows through it. Many people have an antagonistic relationship with their body. They judge their body; they try to constantly make their body into something it's not. Many people suffer from body hate and shame. Some may even try to force their body to do things that can be painful or even harmful. As a result, they may not give their body what it really needs: true nourishment.

Your body is a reflection of your consciousness.

In Sura Flow, you can start a conversation with your body simply by paying attention. You can raise your energy consciousness by listening to your body. Pay close attention to what your body communicates to you. When you reject or neglect your body, you separate yourself from the wisdom of your own body, your primary vehicle of creation. The key is to stop shaming, controlling, and hating your physical body. It's important to learn how to accept and love yourself as you are now. This simple yet profound act allows your body to become the healthiest version of itself.

In spiritual practice, it's essential to take care of your body. It's constantly performing vital functions that you don't even have to think about. Your body can take on a lot, but it also holds stress and trauma. This can show up as pain, tension, and even disease. Eckhart Tolle coined the term "pain-body" to describe where you store past, unfelt, painful emotions. Flow meditation gives you an opportunity to feel and release these past experiences. When you feel, you heal. When you take time to pay attention to your body, you give yourself an opportunity to release past hurts and return to balance.

Healing happens when you stop rejecting the parts of your body you dislike or feel bad about and take time to be present with all parts of yourself. Society has taught us to hate our bodies by constantly promoting unattainable shapes and sizes. This keeps many of us in the loop of body shame. From the time we're born, we're constantly being sent messages from the media, and even the people around us, about what the standard of beauty is. This conditioned way of thinking is what we've unnaturally adopted as an impossible target. It keeps us in a state of constant suffering.

*When you feel,
you heal.*

It's important to be aware of these unrealistic standards while engaging in a mindful body practice. Give yourself permission to release these conditioned ideas from your mind — even on a daily basis, if needed. Sometimes you need to remind yourself to be kind to yourself every day and learn to love yourself and your body again and again. Your body is an extension of your energy. Take time to feed it with positive attention and care.

Loving Your Body as a Path to Awakening

Your body is a divine instrument. Through it, you create your divine desires. Your body also guides you. When your body tenses and tightens up, it's a signal. Your body is experiencing stress. It's signaling fear or a negative resistant response, such as "no." Notice what your body is really telling you when it contracts.

When your body relaxes, it's a positive sign you can use in your life path. It means that you feel receptive and open. You feel good. It can also signify an intuitive "yes." Your body is constantly speaking to you moment-to-moment. It's a valuable, real-time biofeedback mechanism through which your spirit also communicates.

Paying attention to your body is an essential practice in meditation. With each thought or emotion you have, it elicits a subtle body response. It could be tension or coherence. By paying attention to these subtleties, you raise your own self-awareness of your body, as well as your thoughts, emotions, and sensations related to the feelings in your body. Bodies change every day, even moment-to-moment. Pay attention to those subtle shifts.

The practice of body awareness can raise and expand your consciousness. When you pay attention to your body, it sends a signal to your brain about your own sensory experiences. Your brain develops the ability to differentiate experiences that can be useful in your spiritual path.

For example, you may notice that when you think about a negative or stressful experience, your body begins to contract or even shut down. Perhaps your solar plexus and shoulders become tight, and your breathing becomes tense. By bringing awareness to that experience, it allows your brain to process the connection: "Thinking about this over and over is not healthy for me. It causes me stress." At that point, you can choose to breathe, self-regulate, or have a new thought experience.

Body awareness empowers you to regulate stress. Consider how many times you've sat at your desk only to find yourself achy in pain. That's probably because you got absorbed in work, and neglected to pay attention to the cues your body was sending you. When you pay attention to the body, it doesn't have to get to the point of pain to know when to take a break. You might notice you feel dehydrated and low energy, so you decide to get up and take a walk to circulate energy through your body. Small actions can help you regulate the amount of stress your body experiences throughout the day.

Another good way to raise body awareness is to practice a body scan. By flowing your awareness through your body, you activate your relaxation response. This allows your body to naturally relax. A body scan gives you an opportunity to heal and return to balance effortlessly. You can practice this technique throughout your day by paying attention to your body sensations and feelings, especially in the lower half and backside of your body (where you tend to lose awareness and sensation). It will not only help you become more present, it will strengthen your mind-body connection.

Practice Feeling Safe in Your Body

A key practice to develop a stronger connection with your physical self is to cultivate safety in your body. When you feel safe in your body, you feel comfortable being in your body. Many people don't feel good or safe in their body, so they tend to abandon being present in it. A good way to practice "body safety" is to turn your attention inward, find those places where you feel pain and tension, and say, "I feel safe here." So for example, if you feel a tightness in your solar plexus, say, "I feel safe in my belly." Keep focusing on that thought and feeling and notice what shifts in your body. You're likely to experience a release of tension, and with that, a greater sense of embodiment.

There's an inner transformation that happens when you choose to relate to all parts of your body with love and acceptance — even if you think your body is ugly, painful, or uncomfortable. The body relaxes. When you relax and accept your body, there's a letting go, a surrender that happens. With that, a movement of energy flows through your physical body. When you're relaxed, more energy moves through your body.

Check in with Yourself:

Notice your relationship with your body. What is it like? Is it antagonistic? Is it loving? Write about it.

Let all your feelings out and bring them to the surface. By becoming fully aware, you can make a clear choice about how you want to feel about your body and develop body awareness.

· How do you feel in your body?
· How do you want to feel in your body?

Once you start relating to your body in an honoring way, it changes your experience of being in your body.

PRACTICE:
Body Awareness

1. With your eyes closed, gently scan your awareness through all parts of your body, starting with your feet.
2. Notice your bodily sensations, how you feel about your body, and the messages your body sends you (such as imbalance, pain, and flow.)
3. Practice compassion and self-acceptance every day toward your body.

74

When you are grounded and secure in your physical body, your meditation can take root and flower open. Through body awareness, you'll learn how to ground your expansive spiritual experiences into your physical being. Integration and embodiment empowers you to make progress and create your deepest desires.

> **Affirmation: I trust and accept my body.**

CHAPTER 8

SEXUALITY AND DESIRE

*"The act of sexual love should by its very nature be
joyous, unconstrained, alive, leisurely, inventive and
full of special delight, which the lovers have learned by
experience to create for one another."*
— **Thomas Merton**

In many traditions, sexuality and desire are taboo or
even "sinful." Desires are considered sacrilegious.
They're called selfish or egoic. Practitioners are taught
to release their desires because they can lead to further
suffering and hindrance on the spiritual path.

Sex is a highly charged subject in the realm of spirituality. The act of sex in religious societies can often
bring up a sense of shame and guilt. This subject tends
to be highly controlled with many rules and limitations. The idea of sex tends to be repressed and is often
distorted. Yet sex is the essence of creating life.

There are spiritual texts that limit, and even assert
abstinence from sex because it can potentially distract
practitioners from their focus on divine attainment.
Control of sexual energy, which is emphasized in
many religious and spiritual texts across the globe,
affects women most acutely.

These ideas have propagated shame when it comes to sex and our sexual body parts — and for no good reason. Men and women are often taught that pleasure is bad. We're told we shouldn't feel it or receive it, and we shouldn't feel good about fully enjoying sex!

The guilt and shame that gets layered on top of sexual pleasure keeps many of us from exploring the full power of our own energy. It keeps our natural feelings repressed. These kinds of negative emotions associated with sex can limit what we're willing to experience. They keep us locked up as a society and as a people. It keeps sexual energy hidden and repressed. Because of that, sex often becomes exploited through dysfunctional and unhealthy means.

In a yin-oriented practice, you accept all aspects of your sexuality and desire as an inherent part of your natural life force energy. Creation springs from desire. When you create anything, it arises from a deeper desire. When you shut down your sexual energy, you shut down a part of yourself. You disconnect from an essential part of who you are. But through skillful awareness, you can learn to harness and channel all aspects of yourself.

Your Natural Desires

In regard to your desires, there's a distinction to be made between higher desires and lower desires. Lower desires bind you. They limit you. They create an experience of bondage and attachment. Addiction is an example of a lower desire, whether it be addiction to sex, money, or food.

Creation springs from desire.

Lower desires come from attachment to certain things and people but only leave a greater sense of void. If you have constant meaningless sex or eat whatever you want all the time, it feels empty. It's like digging into a bottomless void. People become addicted to things that don't truly serve them. Indulging lower desires over and over again limits you. It creates further bondage and disconnection and divides you from your spirit.

Higher desires connect you to your spirit. They provide you with love and freedom. They are sacred. Higher desires bring you closer to your true self. Take, for example, the desire to be of service, which can uplift you and make you feel deeply connected to others. Higher desires inspire.

They make you more loving, creative, and passionate. A higher desire comes from a place of love. It makes you better. Higher desires help you grow. You become more compassionate, more connected, and balanced.

Divine desires are important. They come from your heart. For example, you might have a desire to connect with God or become self-realized. Your desires feed your creations and actions. They exist for a reason. You can trust higher desires. You need no one's permission or validation to trust your inner desires. Your higher desires exist for a reason.

> *Higher desires connect you to your spirit.*

Without feeling and desire, actions are empty. If you act on the mind alone, it has a completely different quality of energy. The energy of passion enlivens your actions. When you restrain your sexuality, you suppress a part of your energy. Your real desire gives you the energy to achieve your goals. It is possible to let your sexuality flow without having to control it. In fact, you can harness your sexual energy to serve your higher desires and your true purpose.

Sexuality is deeply connected to creativity, your creative life force energy. Your sexual energy *is* life force energy. Passion is the fuel, the furnace that drives creative inspirations. It is completely natural that in the depth of your own spiritual rapture you feel this intense sexual energy rising. Some people refer to it as kundalini energy.

Kundalini in Sanskrit means "coiled snake," and it's located at the base of the spine. In Hinduism, it refers to the divine feminine energy. It is pure life force energy. When this energy awakens, it can also awaken the power of your sexual force. This force is activating.

You can channel your sexual energy to help promote your own health, creativity, and well-being. It can become an elixir that nourishes your health and radiance. Sexual life force energy can be healing and regenerative when it's allowed to flow. It is possible to learn how to skillfully channel your sexual energy.

PRACTICE:
Being Present with Your Desires

1. Take time to sit with your desires, all of your desires. Notice the feeling tone between your higher and lower desires. Where do you feel them in your body? What are they telling you?
2. Become aware of the unconscious beliefs you have about your own desires and your sexuality.
3. What would it be like if you surrendered to your divine desires?

Passion and purpose are driven by our deeper desires. Oprah said, *"Passion is energy. Feel the power that comes from focusing on what excites you."* To truly develop your practice, it's vital to engage in activities and work that inspire you. A good spiritual practice is to do something every day that brings you joy — just for the sake of pure joy.

Your true joy springs from a deeper desire. When you engage in the things that make you feel passion, purpose, and joy, you activate your energy and full potential. You come to know what it means to live in union with your divine spirit. Acting on your deeper desires is a spiritual practice.

> **Affirmation: My desires are beautiful.
> I trust my sexual energy and allow it to flow.**

CHAPTER 9

EMOTIONS

*"Accepting means you allow yourself to feel whatever
it is you are feeling at that moment.
It is part of the isness of the Now. You can't argue with
what is. Well, you can, but if you do, you suffer."*
— **Eckhart Tolle**

We are emotional beings. As humans, we feel a wide range of emotions from love to fear. They are a major aspect of our existence. Yet emotions and feelings are often overlooked as an important part of the spiritual path. We often hear, "Your emotions are just temporary." It's a comment that tends to disregard our deeper emotions, as if they are only secondary. Some may even view them as an obstacle to spiritual enlightenment or "being spiritual." In today's society, there's a negative connotation that comes with being "too emotional."

Since people often recoil from the idea of emotionality, the tendency is to try to control our emotions. However, there's a difference between mastery and control. When we try to control our emotions, what we're really doing is repressing them. The energy of control restricts. It pushes and forces. Control doesn't allow energy to flow. When we suppress our emotions without letting them move, they become trapped in the body-mind, and those repressed emotions (wounds) unconsciously drive our behaviors and choices, often acted out by the ego.

In meditation, it's common to push painful emotions away in an effort to be peaceful. But the way to peace is *through* the pain. What's needed is the ability and safety to fully feel, most especially the pain. Once we feel and experience our emotions, without judgment, we find it's easier to release them. Feeling and owning our true emotions takes courage. It gives us the opportunity to become intimate with who we really are.

Your practice helps you heal the divide between what you're *really feeling* and what you think you *should be feeling*. These subtle inner conflicts create mental and physical tensions. Through continued practice, you'll begin to give yourself permission to feel what you really feel and release those tensions with ease. This empowers you to find a way to release the disconnection between thoughts and feelings. By having this awareness, you can discover a heightened sense of congruence in your life where your intentions, thoughts, feelings, and desires are aligned.

Mastering your emotions takes the willingness to really be with them, exactly the way they are. It means you're not afraid to experience your emotions, no matter how crazy, chaotic, or dark they may seem. Feeling emotions can be a messy experience, but there's no filter in meditation. It's a time to be fully intimate and present with all of your emotions. When you develop emotional awareness, you become more comfortable with the full range of your own emotions — both light and dark. You allow yourself to fully feel, no matter what. This becomes your secret superpower.

Spiritual Beliefs in Dealing with Emotions

In some teachings, there's a perception that in spiritual practice you've got to transcend negative emotion in order to reach enlightenment. "You are more than your emotions" is a commonly heard phrase, yet it creates an unnecessary expectation that you're supposed to get past all the painful, yucky emotions in order to be considered "spiritual." It's unfortunate, but when emotional bypassing happens, you're not provided with the real resources you need to heal your own unconscious emotional wounding.

Transcendence can inadvertently lead people to spiritual bypassing by prematurely abandoning and denying their true emotions in an effort to "transcend." This often leads to the denial of unfelt, repressed emotion in order to be in a "higher" transcended state. Instead of doing the deeper work of healing, meditation practitioners focus on peace and positivity; in effect disowning their own shadow.

At times, practitioners are encouraged to "be present" and feel their emotions, but even with this suggestion, it's implied as a way to "move beyond them." Again, emotions are treated as a secondary process instead of a way to spiritually evolve.

It's Okay to Be Emotional

Today, "being emotional" often has a negative connotation. It implies you're unstable, even weak. It tends to be associated with women since they're naturally more emotional. In Western culture, logic and intellectual thinking tend to be valued over feelings and emotions.

Emotions, however, are deeply valuable. They are "energy in motion." They contain information that can help raise your consciousness. When you have an emotional response, you can listen and pay attention. Even when you have a negative emotion, it's valuable information.

For example, anxiety could be a warning signal telling you, "you're not in the right place," or "something is wrong." Jealousy can point to what you really want to create for yourself. If you were taught to constantly ignore or disregard your own emotions and instead get to the happy place, you can end up doing yourself a grave disservice.

The real work in meditation is being real with yourself. It means you're willing to look at your own shadow. It's the courage to dive into your uncomfortable, dark emotions. This calls you to "descend" right into your emotional body and feel all that's true for you. When you learn how to lean into your deeper, darker emotions instead of avoiding them, you embody your truth. This skill of being present with all that arises, just as it is, empowers you to experience true spiritual and emotional health.

We as a society tend to feel uncomfortable with hard emotions. The discomfort we feel is often met by a basic stress response, flight or fight. We *avoid* what we feel or we *act out*.

For the majority of us, the tendency is to avoid our deeper emotions through distraction and withdrawal. This is the flight response. We might do this by keeping ourselves overly busy. Ways we engage the flight response may look like self-isolation, attaching ourselves to our electronic devices, or overeating.

The real work in meditation is being real with yourself.

Avoidance represses the core emotion and embeds it in our energy and body. It keeps us in a constant dysfunctional loop with the object of our attachment, whether it's binge-watching TV, overworking, or some other distraction. Today there are so many ways to distract ourselves from what we truly feel inside. We only need to pick up our phones to disconnect from the deeper internal experiences we're having.

When we feel bad, we may unconsciously act out. This is the fight response. We get triggered — someone does something that reminds us of a past wound and we get upset. Because of this, we may get angry or even violent. We have an immediate reaction. We place blame and hurt feelings on others. This, unfortunately, has led to worldwide violence and war. When this happens, instead of being present with deeper uncomfortable emotions, we keep them repressed, and their focus remains external. Those misguided efforts lead toward further dominance and control.

It's important to become aware of what drives you when it comes to uncomfortable emotions. Sometimes, when people feel bad, it keeps them from sitting on the cushion. Anxiety is often a result of repressing and denying deeper feelings. When people feel anxious and stressed, it becomes incrementally harder to sit, especially if they're unaware of how they're dealing with their uncomfortable feelings.

The world would be a different place if men and women felt safe enough to be vulnerable and express their uncomfortable feelings and emotions. We need to create safe spaces, particularly for men and young boys, to connect with their feelings. As a society, we need to provide resources for people to release their stress and express their sadness. What's needed now more than ever is emotional healing and development, for both men and women.

Emotional Healing is Key to Developing Resilience

Meditation teaches us another way: to fully allow emotions and experience them without judgment.

Emotions are a natural part of our human experience. There is no need to try to get rid of bad emotions in order to achieve a positive emotional state. Paradoxically, it's by feeling bad emotions that we're able to experience a higher baseline of inner peace.

We need a more authentic approach. You may notice that as you develop your meditation, you encounter intense emotions from your past experiences. When you raise the energy of your practice to a place of peace, everything that contains a denser vibration will naturally come to the surface in order to be released. These memories and experiences bubble up for a reason. It's an opportunity to resolve and heal from past painful experiences.

These old wounds come to visit because you've made space to feel. It's natural to experience difficult and dark emotions when you sit in meditation. When you take time to just be, you'll begin to feel the deeper truths and feelings emerge within your being. Meditation is an opportunity to cleanse and truly come to balance with past hurts. By being completely present with your emotions, without trying to get past them or rid of them, you heal them.

If you have the courage to experience them fully, and express them in a healthy way, you'll discover a greater sense of wholeness and ease.

PRACTICE:
Compassion Toward Your Emotions
As They Are

1. Experience your feelings as they are. Let your emotions flow without trying to get rid of them, make them wrong, or change them.

2. Admit your true feeling, whatever it is. You can say it loud or write it down. You may notice a release of energy when speaking the truth of your experience.

3. Let yourself feel what you truly feel. Remember, *feeling is healing*.

4. Make space to experience your dark, challenging emotions.

5. Send yourself loving kindness and acceptance when you're feeling negative emotions. Say to yourself, "I accept what I feel" and send yourself compassion.

Instead of suppressing, changing, and transcending your feelings through spiritual practice, go into the center of your darkest fears and emotions. This is the way to true liberation. It may seem scary. You may secretly fear you'll get lost or overpowered by dark emotions like grief. But in avoiding hard emotions, you become imprisoned by them.

The way out is the way through. Go into the center of your pain. That's where you'll experience real energy transformation. That's where you'll find your true power and unleash pure energy. Flow meditation gives you the courage to face what you feel.

Trust that you'll come out on the other side once you've authentically connected to your true emotions. In fully allowing your emotions and feelings, you become free. It's possible to learn how to harness your emotions and skillfully transform them through self-compassion.

When you allow real space for what you truly feel, you connect to your true self. Through continued practice of being present with your deeper feelings, there is profound opportunity for emotional development and healing. The more you meditate, the more you develop your emotional intelligence through self-awareness.

When you let emotions surface, experience them fully, and observe them with compassion, you are no longer prisoner to your intense, uncomfortable feelings. It's important to be aware that's going to happen in meditation and to fully allow it. By giving yourself permission to fully feel, you can experience a release and eventually a resolution of old emotional baggage.

By connecting to your deeper emotions, you become more connected to yourself. The moment you begin to shut down or invalidate your feelings, or try to change them superficially, you deny your own true experience. It is okay to trust what you feel. When you validate what you feel and let yourself fully experience it, you become wholly available to life.

In Sura Flow meditation, you learn to become intimate with your feelings. Feelings exist for a reason and your emotions are important. They contain information about yourself. It's also the way your higher-self speaks to you. A change in your emotional feeling tone can indicate a vital sign about your life trajectory. When you tune into your life path and the direction you want to experience, you may feel an emotion arise, like joy. Lower emotions tend to indicate a less authentic path. Higher heart-felt emotions, like natural excitement and passion, are often positive signs that you're headed in the right direction.

Emotions are subtle. They communicate in a multitude of ways. They may be telling you what you need to heal and what you need to listen to. They may even guide you through your intuition. You cannot experience higher emotions, like joy and contentment, without allowing yourself to feel the lower emotions, like pain and grief. All these feelings move through the same gateway of the human emotional blueprint.

When you don't allow your emotions and feelings, you don't allow a natural conduit of energy to flow. When you cry, water releases from your eyes. Water is a natural conduit of energy. It's healing. When you shut down your emotions or invalidate them by saying, "I shouldn't feel that," you invalidate your true experience and trap those pent-up emotions in your body. By listening to your emotions and honoring them, you connect back to yourself. You become more whole, more embodied. You find deeper healing and meaning which allows you to grow.

Your emotions are the channel through which you feel and experience the divine. It is not just through the thinking mind that you experience God. There is a deep emotional feeling and connection when you're in union with the divine. It's an energy experience that extends beyond words and thought. It is the energy of love.

Emotions are an incredible, phenomenal aspect of the human experience. They can also help you create your deepest desires. When you let yourself feel the emotional power and joy of your creations, you're more likely to realize them. To allow your emotions is to allow the full expression of your divine self, your true self. Letting yourself fully feel is the act of being alive.

Remember, there's no expectation to be peaceful. Sometimes, you have to get through the chaos and darkness to reach the light. Sometimes, meditation is a raw, messy, chaotic inner experience. This is a painful but necessary part of the journey. Don't skip any steps or glaze over uncomfortable experiences. Be true to what's arising in the moment. It will serve you in the long run and help you truly heal.

Return to Balance

Healing and expressing your true emotions leads to wholeness and balance. Emotions are directly related to your health. In Chinese medicine, disease is seen as the result of imbalanced emotions. These imbalanced emotions can be examined in different parts of the body and can even lead to physical disease. The repression of these emotions can also manifest as stress and anxiety. This is why emotional health is paramount to your own well-being and resilience.

You can tap into your deeper emotions through meditation, writing, and creative expression, such as art. It's important to find a healthy way to express your emotions. Singing, dancing, improv, and community connection are wonderful ways to share and express yourself. By developing true emotional awareness, you also develop your emotional intelligence. This process increases your energy flow. Emotional development is a key component in personal growth that can lead you toward higher levels of compassion and understanding.

> **Affirmation: My emotions are valuable.
> I am willing to feel them and pay attention
> to them.**

CHAPTER 10

ENERGY

"The more willing you are to surrender to the energy within you, the more power can flow through you."
— **Shakti Gawain**

Everything is energy. You are made of pure energy. This is also referred to as *chi* or *prana*. It is your creative life force energy. Energy exists all around us and within us. It's what all matter is made of. You may not see energy, but you may sense it. Universal energy flows through all of creation. It is unlimited. It's possible to tap into this universal energy flow and use it to heal and develop yourself.

Chi is the subtle electromagnetic energy that runs through your body like a superhighway system. The main source of chi is your breath. Without it, you cannot survive. By learning how to breathe more fully, you can increase your energy levels. When you are chronically stressed and breathing in a shallow and fast manner, you are depleting your chi force and connection to your Source. In this state, it's harder to connect intuitively and be truly open.

Your creative life force energy contains divine intelligence. The more you connect to it, the better it can serve you. You can connect to it consciously with your breath. Taking longer and slower breaths increases your chi. It's your energy intelligence that guides and protects you. It silently directs you in the right way if you listen. Some people may refer to it as "God." Others call it "Love" or the "The Way."

*Your creative
life force energy
contains divine
intelligence.*

In Chinese medicine, your body has meridians, like channels that flow energy throughout your body. When these meridians are blocked, it creates "dis-ease" and tension. Those deeper inner tensions come from blocked emotional wounds. These are stressful, traumatizing experiences that weren't felt and expressed at the time but became trapped in the body as energy.

One of the main aims in Flow practice is to open your energy. You do this when you clear your past emotional and energetic blocks. In opening your chi, you become open to embodying your spiritual self. This is the process of awakening, which includes opening and cleansing your energy. When your energy is running smoothly throughout your body, you experience health and vitality.

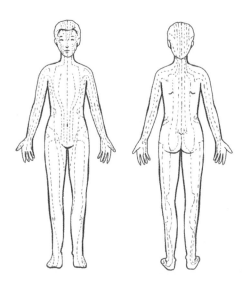

Example of Energy Meridians

When you're relaxed, your muscles are more open and your chi energy flows naturally through your body — you feel healthy and balanced. When it gets stuck or imbalanced, you may experience pain, "disease," and discomfort. Stress is essentially blocked chi and is signified by tension. It's energy that hasn't been released or moved. Healthy free flow of energy is connected to every aspect of your being: your emotions, mental state, physical state, environment, relationships, and more.

It is possible to release old energy blocks and past wounds through Flow practice. The first step is to become aware of them. Each wound has an entire energy experience that contains a story, feelings, emotions, meanings, and an electrical charge. It explains why you tend to attract the same experience that brings continual pain and suffering. Think of it as a magnet lodged deep within your unconscious energy. It's continually "attracting" the outer experience that triggers your deepest core wounds. This often includes the most common negative emotions, such as shame, betrayal, and fear of abandonment.

As a human, you have endured trauma. We have all endured some form of trauma. Some of us have suffered from deeper traumatic experiences than others, which affects the way we function in daily life. Sometimes we are not even aware that our past experiences are negatively affecting our present moment.

Sura Flow helps us raise our awareness of our unconscious and subconscious tendencies, which primarily drive the way we perceive, interact, and orient in life. Our conscious mind contains a small portion of our creative energy. However, the more self-aware we become, the more we can shed light on our own unconscious and subconscious tendencies that may cause us to act out of fear or trauma. We can receive access to these areas of our consciousness by paying attention to our somatic (body) response, our nervous system, our breathing, and our energy. When we feel a contraction and reaction, it often signifies a need for balance and neutrality, to neutralize past triggers and wounds.

It's one thing to sit in meditation; it's another to learn how to clear your past energy wounds. Sura Flow helps you tap into your deeper unconscious and subconscious tendencies that keep you stuck in a pattern.

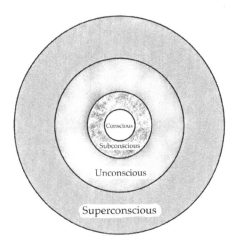

The majority of your experiences are influenced by your subconscious and unconscious mind that are often hidden from the conscious mind. These experiences have been predominantly created from your earliest life experiences and what you learned from your parents, teacher, and peers. They are conditions that cause you to automatically think, feel, and believe what you do.

When you act from the unconscious or subconscious, you may be acting from a limited place. It can knock you into survival mode so that you stay safe. We naturally develop ways to navigate and relate in life, but when your pain constantly drives your life choices, you experience the same pattern of suffering again and again. When a pain-body becomes crystallized by past unfelt wounds, there is a denser, more formed ego in place that reacts strongly when it is challenged.

Sura Flow helps you tap into your deeper unconscious and subconscious tendencies that keep you stuck in a pattern.

The ego needs control and can be fragile when confronted. A strong emotional reaction is often a sign of the ego's fragility. The ego survives through denial, which is one of the biggest obstacles to healing. Some people describe a strong ego formed from fear-based reality as having a heavy vibration.

Your practice empowers you to release the edges and identifications of the ego. It raises your vibration by giving you the tools to release the heavy hurts of past pains. It gives you access to a larger space, your superconscious mind (your divine intelligence). In this transcendent state, you can see the true nature of reality or "the essence of the Universe." By connecting to your Source energy through Flow, you're empowered to release past energetic impressions that keep you from experiencing the fullness of your joy.

Meditation is not enough for clearing the deeper energetic wounded patterns we all have. This is because they are very deep. These wounds lie in the unconscious realm, they are hard to recognize — we cannot see our own blind spots.

Clearing patterns and experiences from the past is very challenging on your own. You can sit in meditation for years and have the same tensions in your body. However, when you work with a practitioner or a group, it is easier to release these deeper energetic patterns. A practitioner can also help identify and clear these past wounds. In a group setting, healing energy becomes amplified. This is because when two or more come together, a stronger flow of energy and transformation can occur.

When your chi is moving, you're in flow with life around you. "Being in the zone" is synonymous with flowing energy. When your chi is flowing, you feel at ease. When your chi is stuck, you experience stress and tension. The key is to be aware of your life force energy and the way it is moving through you. When your inner energy is balanced, there's a quality of energy moving through your life that feels aligned and at peace, even when things are challenging. You know when you're in flow, and you know when you're off and stuck.

Your chi contains valuable information and intelligence. When you learn to listen to it in meditation, you benefit in myriad ways. For example, pay attention to the way energy flows in the different areas of your life. Where the chi is stagnant or stuck, you tend to experience stress. It can manifest as low energy, frustration, and/or unhealthy patterns. Where the chi is flowing, you experience abundance, peace, and contentment. Effortless flow teaches you to pay attention to all forms of energy.

Divine flow expresses itself through energy.

When you pay attention to your chi, you can circulate it through your physical body, further promoting physical health. You may have seen these practices, such as qigong or tai chi, where slow, flowing, graceful movements promote chi flow. Through effortless flow, it's possible to gather this chi and use it toward a higher purpose, such as self-healing, or even healing others. You can harness chi like a laser or keep it open like a receptive vessel. When you need to get things done, it will feel better to make your chi more focused, contained, and purposeful.

Energy is the universal language of spirit. When you're aware of energy, you're aware of the interconnectedness of life. Divine flow expresses itself through energy.

The more you meditate, the more aware you become of energy. It is possible to tap into this deeper flow through your practice. When you listen to the deeper energy movement in your life, you feel more in tune with all of life. You may also notice that you show up at the right time, at the right place.

Living in Balance

Wu wei in Chinese means "effortless action." It is considered a noble action that arises from "doing nothing." You are at peace, even when you're doing. It is possible to complete actions while you are in a state of oneness, even amid challenges and frenetic activity. It's about letting go of the rigid ways of control and ego so you can yield spontaneously to the true demands and needs of the moment.

When you are disconnected, you feel frazzled, fragmented. In this state, you may be moving at a rushed, uneven pace in your life. This can cause further stress and angst. Your mind is in the future, but your body is in the moment. This quality of your energy is also reflected in your chi.

Your energy radiates from your physical body to the biofield around you, also known as an aura. For example, you can visibly tell when someone has healthy, balanced energy. There is a sense of wholeness and fullness that is present. This is what is referred to as a "high" vibration. Positive chi flow has a quality that is easy, light, open, and free.

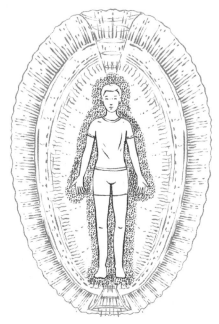

Energy Aura

While working with energy, the intention is to raise it. You can learn to harness universal energy, the natural energy that flows through all of existence. Everything has energy and vibrates at its own frequency. Your vibration can shift moment-to-moment. The more aware you are, the more conscious you become of your own frequency. You can shift the energetic nature of yourself and others by developing your chi. This is one of the core practices of Sura Flow: refining your energy.

Energy Healing

In Sura Flow, you learn how to consciously restore your energy. Some people refer to this as energy healing or balancing. You are made of energy and can therefore channel energy to yourself and others. During effortless flow, you can place your hands on your heart and belly and consciously send extra energy to those centers of your body. You will notice that afterward, you feel more restored.

When you're aware of your energy, you know how to clear and rejuvenate your energy through practices such as grounding. With grounding, you utilize visualization by imagining being grounded like a big tree with roots growing into the earth. You can envision running the Earth's energy through your body, clearing and cleansing it of any toxins, then nourishing your body with the Earth's healing energy. When practiced consistently, this visual practice has immediate positive rejuvenating effects.

Healing your energy begins with intention. When you are connected to your chi, you're connected to your spirit. You feel fully engaged. You are alive and energetic. There is a divine spark inside you when you're connected to your chi. The ancient masters and angels are often depicted with a halo of light. This is a depiction of their chi — the radiance and energy that is activated in their aura by spiritual enlightenment. This expression of chi is also reflected by a light or clarity in the eyes. Your eyes express your soul. With flowing chi, it is easy to smile, to express yourself, and to live with purpose.

Energy healing is the practice of releasing subtle blocks in the body that keep your natural chi from flowing. You can experience healing in the following ways.

1. Hands-on healing (on yourself)
2. Aura healing (of the biofield around you)
3. Long-distance healing (such as prayer or focused intention)
4. Through meditation (relaxation and visualization)

Healing your energy begins with intention.

Many people are aware of energy healing today from the practice of Reiki. Reiki also uses universal energy. It is a more well-known traditional form of energy healing that includes initiations and symbols.

When I was in Thailand in 2005, I became a Reiki master. It was a profound experience that opened me to the healing arts. I am deeply grateful for the experience of learning Reiki. However, with time and experience teaching, I realized no initiations or symbols were necessary to practice energy healing. When I started teaching this in Los Angeles at the request of my yoga students, the healing energy automatically flowed when a group gathered for the intention of healing. That was when I realized that healing energy is available to all of us at any time.

We all have natural healing energy to tap into. It is an inherent part of who we are. While many people today still practice and benefit from Reiki, I believe we are moving past these traditional forms of energy healing that require external initiations. More and more people are realizing that we no longer need exclusive forms of healing from an outside source to activate our own internal power. You can discover and trust your innate gifts by developing your own practice and working with people you trust.

Energy healing is beneficial in many ways. It helps you feel more clear, present, and centered. The more you heal from past wounds, the more present you become. It clears a space in your psyche to be open to new information. Healing gives you a way to discharge stress from your nervous system. Free of stress and lower vibrations from unconscious wounding, you're more clear to receive intuitive insights. Healing also helps you develop your intuition. It promotes flow in your everyday life and helps you feel more powerful in your center.

When you're healing and moving old energy, you may notice some of the following symptoms. These symptoms can also arise during a Flow meditation practice. They are a result of detoxifying yourself of old emotions and energy. Healing often consumes energy and requires rest and sometimes extra calories. Your body is re-calibrating to a new inner-balance.

Always be sure to consult a medical professional if you have any concerns about your health.

Healing symptoms:

- Fatigue and extreme exhaustion
- Aches and pains
- Old emotions
- Changes in energy
- Disruption in sleep
- Inability to think clearly due to tiredness
- Tingling and/or heat/cold sensations
- Headaches
- Digestive changes
- Nausea
- Low energy
- Dark and uncomfortable emotions/feelings
- Feeling blissful

It can take twenty-four hours to a week or more to integrate healing energy. The best thing to do is to rest as much as possible and drink plenty of water. Stay quiet and do your best not to mingle in populated areas with many different energies. You can take actions to help integrate new energy.

Integrate healing energy by:

- Spending time in nature
- Spending time in solitude
- Journaling about your experience
- Resting and sleeping
- Practicing restorative yoga
- Taking a hot Epsom salt bath
- Swimming in the ocean
- Walking barefoot on the earth
- Sitting under a tree
- Lying on the earth

After releasing old energy and integrating new energy, you will feel:

- More clear
- Aligned
- Brighter
- Focused
- Energized
- Renewed
- Limitless
- More creative
- More intuitive
- More in flow
- Stronger mind-body connection
- Higher energy/vibration

Cultivate and Harness Your Chi

In Sura Flow meditation, you learn how to cultivate your chi when you meditate. During your practice, you can open up to universal energy and allow it to fill and restore you. In this state, you are receptive to the sweet nectar meditation has to offer. It's a blissful sensation that's calming, and it often comes with wisdom.

In energy healing, you are releasing old, stagnant energy and inviting in new, fresh chi. You can imagine drawing in positive energy from your environment or from nature. You can call your own energy back into your body in the form of a golden sun. If you want to imagine that your energy is already within you, you can affirm your energy at your heart center and allow it to expand outward into your aura. Energy healing is simply bringing your energy into balance.

In your Sura Flow practice, you are doing more than just sitting; you're gathering your life force energy and learning how to channel and direct it. You're developing knowledge of your own energy by listening to it. By getting in touch with your energy, you can learn how to harness it and have more energy as a result.

You can become skillful with your life force energy and learn how to slow down the effects of aging and cultivate longevity. Through practice, you can tap into the deeper wisdom of your chi. When you pay close attention to what bolsters and drains your energy, you will understand one of the great keys to life.

PRACTICE:
Tune in to Your Creative Life Force Energy

1. What boosts or drains your energy?
2. What is your life force energy telling you?
3. What kind of energy would you like to cultivate?

The more in touch you are with your energy, the more energy you can generate. In Sura Flow, you learn how to raise your awareness of energy so you can develop your chi. You can increase your energy through consistent Flow practices like grounding and balancing. You can also learn how to flow your energy through relaxation and healing practices.

Energy healing is simply bringing your energy into balance.

Be mindful of keeping your energy "fresh and pure" whether it is in your body or your home space. Maintaining positive chi means keeping things balanced, healthy, and clean. The words you say, the company you keep, the work you do, the food you eat... these things are all part of your energy system. Be aware of the quality of energy you are creating every day and in all aspects of your life.

Essentially, you are raising your energy (your vibration). This doesn't mean being high in the sky but rather grounded, awake, and alert. When the quality of your energy is high, it is easier to be present. It is easier to live as your pure, authentic self.

> **Affirmation: I am aware of
> my life force energy.
> It guides me in the right direction.**

CHAPTER 11

INTEGRITY

*"Integrity is doing the right thing,
even when no one is watching."*
— **Charles Marshall**

Integrity becomes a natural way of life as you develop yourself. The purpose of meditation is self-realization. The more you sit in stillness and witness the nature of your mind, the more self-aware you become. Through increased self-awareness, you begin to realize the nature of your true self. The purpose of Flow practice is to know yourself. In this way, you become more and more yourself. You realize that everything you need is within you.

As you develop your practice and begin to release old ways of thinking and being, you'll find yourself becoming more discerning in the ways you spend your time and attention. You think more deeply about what you are engaging in. The things you enjoyed in the past may no longer satisfy you the way they did before. You find that your preferences change.

With continued spiritual development, you're likely to experience this in all aspects of your life, from the food you eat, to your daily routine, to the people you connect with. You're becoming more conscious of what you're creating and the place you are creating from. It becomes clearer to you when you're creating from a place of love versus fear.

Trust what you want to experience on a deeper level.

You might find that old relationships start to shift or fall away. With this there is often a new space of uncharted territory. Some people experience it as a profound sense of loneliness or emptiness. It can also arise as "the dark night of the soul." However, it can be a time of marked solitude for greater healing and personal development. This space is often necessary to attain higher levels of self-awareness.

This time of change in many ways can feel like a loss. It *is* a loss. It's a loss of your old self. You could say, the loss of your ego. The things you have identified strongly with may have gone away. This could be your job role or the things you used to enjoy. It's normal to grieve the loss of things you once had. Give yourself the space to acknowledge what is part of your past and to feel what you really feel. It's okay to feel the sadness.

You might find that certain activities, such as shopping or busyness, don't feel as engaging as they once were. Whatever this change may be, embrace it. Trust what you want to experience on a deeper level. If needed, find healthy ways to communicate how you want to spend your time and energy.

Your internal changes may push you to express new boundaries in your relationships. As people in your life begin to sense your growth and transformation, you might experience resistance or even pushback from loved ones. People who are close to you may question your newfound sense of direction. Perhaps they're not accustomed to the new you. Stay calm and know that these kinds of tensions and resistances are normal. When it happens, return to your center and ground yourself. Remember compassion for yourself and others as you tread new territory.

As you progress in your practice, you might have deeper realizations about the nature of your work and your relationships. These honest insights may at first feel jarring because some of them might require real, meaningful change that's scary to make. Take time to be with them and give yourself the time and space to move at your own pace. Trust these inner changes, though at first they may be very uncomfortable.

You will naturally transform through consistent Flow practice. It's a continual attunement toward balance. Through practice, you're undergoing a constant process of purification. Energy flow helps you to release old egoic patterns and to embrace your spiritual self, your authentic self. You become aligned inside. With these internal changes, you'll notice that you begin to make life choices from a deeper, felt sense. It is from this internal alignment that you begin to develop your own sense of what is right and what is wrong for you.

The more you practice, the more personal integrity becomes a natural part of your life. Being one with your word, speaking the truth, engaging in right livelihood; all these things become vital to the way you live. You become more conscious of how you spend your time and energy. Aligned ways of living and being becomes a way of life. Living a high energy life supports you and allows you to support others.

With continued practice, you develop a reverence for all of life, including plants, animals, nature, and everyone around you. You understand the deep interconnectedness of all life forms and how energy flows through every part of life, from a tiny insect to the cosmos.

You come to understand on a deep level that "right action" allows you to live in harmony in life. That it's more than being a good boy or girl who follows the rules. It's a way of living that exemplifies personal excellence and integrity. You know when you are living your right path because your choices and actions benefit the whole.

PRACTICE:
Personal Reflection on Values

1. What is most important to you?
2. What offers you a personal sense of what is "right?"
3. What positive qualities do you want to nurture in yourself?

Developing your innate ethical nature allows you to progress. By aligning yourself with truth and balance, you nurture your chi. You come to know virtue, your own moral excellence. Virtue increases your energy flow.

As you purify your consciousness and release internal blocks and tensions, you increase your spiritual power. You become more the person you are meant to be. You evolve into a clear channel, a mirror, and a guide. Divine energy flows with ease when you develop your inner self. This includes your healing and intuitive gifts.

Virtue increases your energy flow.

In today's Western world, humility and virtue are not necessarily a primary focus in many spiritual practices. But they are qualities that anyone can develop. Through practice, you cultivate your own consciousness. With this, a quality of energy begins to imbue your body and mind. It follows your actions and your intentions. You find that the intentions you create from your pure, innermost self manifest with more ease and grace. You live your true, authentic self.

There are three essential practices that bolster your sense of self and help you cultivate energy flow. Keep these practices in mind as you develop your Flow practice to increase your confidence.

Practice: Self-compassion

When you're learning and practicing meditation, it's vital to be free of self-judgment and criticism. It's easy to fall into thinking you're not good enough at practice or even to judge yourself for being judgmental. What dispels stress, judgment, and negative thinking is the perspective of compassion. The practice of loving kindness and forgiveness every day will bolster your Sura Flow practice.

Self-compassion gives you the energy space to focus in a positive way. As soon as you begin building compassionate awareness, the *way* you think changes. It creates spaciousness. When you have kindness for yourself, it's easier to have compassion toward others. This simple yet powerful skill releases subtle tensions within the self and also with others. This is why it's highly effective to practice compassion every day. Let loving kindness be your foundation for your Flow practice and you will feel supported in being your true self.

Practice: Self-love

The active practice of self-love allows you to heal and return to balance. More than treating yourself to nice things, self-love is about providing yourself with the nourishment and energetic support to thrive. Many of us did not receive the unconditional love we needed as children. Because of that, we often unconsciously search for external forms of love and attention. In developing your own practice, you understand that the love you truly need is already inside you.

It takes practice, but it's possible to learn how to love yourself by caring for yourself as you would a best friend or small child. Consider who you were as a child, what you really wanted, and what you truly needed. Provide yourself with all that you needed as a small child. Give yourself the energy, love, and attention you need to feel safe and secure. You can display a picture of yourself as a child and consciously send yourself love.

You can learn how to create new healthy patterns by practicing conscious loving actions toward yourself. For example, make decisions from a place of self-love. Ask yourself, "If I really loved myself, what would I do?" When you make choices from a place of uncon-ditional self-love, you align yourself to your Source energy. This way of being becomes a natural guide for living your best life. When you know how to love and

cherish yourself, you naturally provide this unconditional loving space of acceptance to others.

*In
developing your
own practice you
understand that the
love you truly need
is already inside
you.*

Practice: Self-nurturing

One of the greatest superpowers you have is the
power of self-nurturing. This is the ability to take
care of yourself so that you can thrive. It contains the
intuitive knowledge of how to best cultivate a space
for growth. This may mean being softer or kinder to
yourself, giving yourself more time to complete tasks,
or taking care of your emotional hurts.

When you begin to shift the focus toward your
inner development, it may mean creating a space
where more boundaries are needed. A boundary may
include a physical space or an amount of time. It can
even be energetic. It's what you need to feel balanced.
Think of it as creating a sacred garden where you have
a fence to keep out predators and weeds. You tend to
the garden so that you can thrive.

Taking care of yourself is not selfish, it's self-
centering. When you are centered and nourished,
you have a greater capacity to create and be present

for others. It's possible that when focusing on others, you may forget about your own well-being. When you understand that you are an integral part of the whole and that your own sense of well-being truly matters, you will develop your practice with the deepest love and respect for yourself.

Personal integrity is a way of living in alignment. This includes the present moment, your relationships, your environment, and all the living beings around you. When you develop virtue, your heart is pure and light. You are free of tension; you are free of worry. You are free to be yourself in the moment.

Affirmation: I surrender to being my true self.

CHAPTER 12

PURPOSE

> *"It is better to live your own destiny imperfectly than*
> *to live an imitation of somebody else's life*
> *with perfection."*
> — **The Bhagavad Gita**

Sura Flow is a way of life. It's a way of living in harmony with life in the present moment. When we accept the present moment, we open ourselves to the creative power of the moment. It isn't enough just to meditate; it's important to take action on the things that give you joy and energy.

When you follow this simple guide of taking action on the things that boost your energy in the moment, you'll find that it naturally leads you exactly where you need to be.

When you listen to your energy and follow your joy, you're likely to experience synchronicity. You find yourself showing up at the right time, at the right place, with the right people. This is a sign of living with the Tao or the energy flow. It is the natural way. You discover an effortless flow. When you pay attention to energy and do what feels right, it leads you to your own destined potential.

We each have a unique life path — *dharma*, which refers to the "right way" of living, or "cosmic law." It includes your life's purpose. Dharma comes from the Sanskrit root word "dhr," which means "hold, maintain, keep." It "keeps" and naturally upholds "cosmic law." When you tap into dharmic living, you can feel the power of aligned living. Flow practice helps you tune into that universal sense of alignment and sustainability.

The more you listen and create from a place of listening, the more attuned you become to your true dharmic path. You find a greater clarity in following your own sense of direction.

When you pay attention to energy and do what feels right, it leads you to your own destined potential.

Meditation is a practice in knowing who you are. The more you sit, the more you become self-aware. The more self-aware you become, the more you do right by yourself by taking action on what's right. When this happens, it unleashes a natural flow. You know when you're living your own true path because you feel yourself living in tandem with all of life. You no longer feel separate but rather an inherent part of existence. You begin to feel you are "living on the mark."

Mythologist and author Joseph Campbell said:

"There's something inside you that knows you're in the center, that knows you're on the beam, that knows you're off the beam. And if you get off the beam to earn money, you've lost your life."

When you're "on the beam," you're likely to feel a sense of flow in your life. With this comes increasing synchronicity, or meaningful coincidences, that lead you in the right direction. Your life takes on a seemingly magical quality where things come together effortlessly and miraculously, better than you could have ever imagined. When you're living your "right path," the universal energy flow is moving with you like wind behind your sails. You'll experience synchronicities that accelerate you toward your own destined path.

This synchronistic way of living becomes more natural the more you learn how to harness chi. Flow is more than sitting and being a good meditator who can meditate for hours in a perfect pose. It's about learning how to experience flow with the energy of the universe. This empowers you to live joyfully and creatively on purpose. Your practice liberates you to live your full self without apology or shame.

It can be a messy path to find your own way. You are creating it from within. Because of this, you won't be able to see the path laid out ahead of you; you have to sense it. But you know it's your own because of how you feel. You feel alive. You experience a deeper joy and connection to all of life. By clearing limiting beliefs and energy blocks, you make way for new possibilities that were once hidden to emerge.

This is how Sura Flow opens you to your life purpose. Discovering your purpose is synonymous with discovering your true self. It's about trusting the inner callings that bring you joy. It gives you courage to take action on what feels right for you. It means trusting in life's unfolding. You trust the universe. And you learn how to trust yourself without needing approval or validation from others.

> *By clearing limiting beliefs and energy blocks, you make way for new possibilities that were once hidden to emerge.*

One of your greatest assets is your attention. It's how you choose to focus your time and energy. Having a positive focus in life is vital to long-lasting happiness. Finding meaning and purpose in what you do helps you develop your energy. It raises your conscious-ness. It motivates you to live better, to do better — for yourself and others. You know when you're living your true potential because it feeds you spiritually.

When you don't have a positive focus in life, it's easy to fall into an unconscious, negative mindset. Without a conscious focus, you become receptive to outer influences. There are many businesses and advertisers that are invested in consuming your attention. With today's innumerable distractions and energy pulls, it serves you to have a positive focus.

If you want to find your passion, I encourage you to do something fun. That may sound simple, but I've discovered that when people allow themselves to have fun, they naturally discover their purpose. Fun opens the space for discovering your true self. Finding passion is a lot like finding love. You find it when you least expect it. You find it when you're open. Let yourself do what you enjoy and your purpose will reveal itself to you naturally.

There can be some blocks to finding your purpose. The first is trying to make your purpose "big and profitable." We're so deeply conditioned as a culture to constantly produce. When you feel pressure to make something "big," you miss the point of experiencing real joy for the sake of joy.

The second block is tied to the first. You think that in order to follow your joy, you need a lot of money or resources. People don't think they deserve to experience fun and joy until *after* they're accomplished or have proven themselves.

Another big block may come from the "demons and dragons" you have to slay along the way. In Joseph Campbell's *Hero's Journey*, he talks about the trials and tribulations along the path to finding your bliss. In this journey, the hero experiences a personal transformation. Whenever you choose to embark on your own unique path, you'll begin to experience forces at play in your life, such as the "unseen thousands of helping hands," when you first begin.

However, as you continue your path, you'll discover that as you begin to harness your own creative power, you come up against major challenges and unconscious forces. This includes both inner and outer forces. It can even include loved ones in your life who resist or create major roadblocks as you attempt to lay the groundwork for your path.

This is why it's important to stay vigilant. Be mindful of who you spend time with, especially when you're creating what's most important to you. It's okay to set healthy boundaries to create the sacred space you need to focus. It's not uncommon that as you develop momentum in your path, you face major upheaval and unexpected obstacles. It's part of growth. Know it's par for the course.

There will be struggles when you set out to achieve your personal vision, but you don't have to succumb to them. Be ready for them. Your practice will prepare you with everything you need to flow with what is. If you're able to persevere, then you can enjoy the final step in the hero's journey: integration back into the real world where you can share your learned gifts with others.

Don't let anything keep you from finding meaning and purpose in your life. Remember, your purpose comes *from* your joy. Abundance can come in any form. It doesn't have to be just money. It can be any resource. Creativity gives you the freedom to create what you want, when you want. When you're looking to live a life of passion and energy, you've got to be truly open.

Your purpose is blissful because you enjoy the process, not just the big end result. When you make it all about money and practicality, the joy spills out. You've got to have space to really explore, make mistakes, be messy, perhaps even be in solitude for a while. Winding, jagged paths led by the heart often lead to wondrous experiences. Your purpose is not just one role; it can shift and continue to evolve.

PRACTICE:
Coaching Questions for Discovering Your Purpose

1. What does it feel like to "live on the mark"? You can imagine this. Where do you feel "it" in your body? Meditate on this sensation and absorb it.
2. What activities cause you to lose track of time?
3. What makes you truly excited?

If you're still exploring passion and purpose as part of your life path, take small steps. Start with simple things like "what would be interesting today?" Learn one new thing a week. Do something different every day. Take yourself out on a date. Create something. Spend time in solitude. Give someone a surprise, like an unexpected compliment or gift. Do anything that breaks you out of your normal comfort zone.

Here are a couple questions to meditate on:

- What would you do if you knew you could not fail?
- What would you do if you had all the time and money in the world?

Living a life of purpose goes hand in hand with Flow practice. It grounds the energy of your spiritual knowledge. When you discover meaning in what you do, you feel connected to the life force energy of the universe. When you live your purpose, it bolsters your health. It boosts your immune system. It makes you feel more resilient and strong in your everyday life. It gives you special energy.

Sura Flow is about following your joy.

Oftentimes, your life purpose is connected to the lives of others. When you work with and serve others, you come to understand the deep interconnectedness and sacredness of life. Being of service to life means being of service to yourself and others. You are part of the whole. When you discover the joy of service, you receive it back manifold.

Your purpose, your passion, and your joy all go hand in hand. They create a positive force field of energy flow in your life. When you listen to and follow what gives you joy, it naturally leads you to your passion and purpose. Joy is an inner guide that creates a quality of energy in your life. It naturally allows you to experience expansion, peace, and contentment. You don't have to get rid of stress; just focus on what brings you joy. This positive force field will elevate you to a whole new level. In this state, you'll discover that stress automatically falls away.

Sura Flow is about following your joy. More than meditation, it's important to laugh, have fun, and fully engage with this experience called life. Be willing to follow the things that feel inherently good for you. Learn how to trust this inner feeling and to follow what feels good for your energy. Joy is a vibration that leads you toward your highest vibrational path.

You'll find that following the inner feeling of joy leads you toward greater synchronicity and purpose. It takes you on a spiritual journey, one that's full of fun, adventure, and growth. Practice isn't about being serious about life. There's levity to be had. When you allow yourself to experience joy, you feel light. You are free. When you're joyful, you're most empowered to be of service to yourself and others.

Synchronicity is a sign that you're living your right path. Trust that it will lead you to your purpose. Remember to take time to enjoy life and to acknowledge and celebrate the sweetness in your life experiences.

Affirmation: I trust what gives me joy.

CHAPTER 13

HEALTH

*"Keep your vitality. A life without health
is like a river without water."*
— Anonymous

Health is a vibration. The more you practice, the more attuned you become to health, balance, and wholeness. Many people today suffer from health challenges. It is not uncommon to have aches, pains, and disease as a human being. However, it's possible to still cultivate health despite any challenge. Flow practice can also help you with your conditions, particularly in providing you with personal resources to self-heal.

You do not have to be in perfect health to create a healthy state of being. Meditation is more than a mental or physical pursuit; it is a holistic practice that touches every part of your life. It affects your life force energy, your emotions, mental state, and overall health. It has the power to offer you more than a peaceful 20-minute session. Flow gives you the ability to raise your energy and improve your health.

The purpose of your practice is to improve your state of health and well-being. To maintain good health, you need the following essential elements:

good exercise, restful sleep, and healthy food. When you practice these basic elements, you balance your energy. Your chi can flow easily through your body. You feel vibrant, fresh, and focused.

When you eat healthy foods from nature, like fruit and vegetables that come from the land, it increases the chi flow in your body. You receive chi from nature. The more pure your diet, the more clear and focused you will feel. Each person has unique dietary needs. I will share what has worked well for me in developing balance and health. However, always consult a professional and your own inner sense for what works best for you.

For the most part, I eat simple organic foods without a lot of ingredients. I eat only when I'm hungry and drink plenty of water. Also, as a personal preference, I don't consume alcohol. Mostly I eat what feels intuitively good for my body. This usually means limiting the amount of dairy and meat products I consume because they tend to slow down the chi flow in the body (they are the two kinds of foods that are often advised by doctors for cancer patients to stop eating).

What I have noticed in myself and others is that food and drinks affect consciousness. They affect your mental clarity. As food moves through your body and your digestive system, it takes energy. It's best to eat an amount that satisfies your appetite and not overeat. Learning how to eat just the right amount will benefit your long-term health. I find that having digestion also supports health and well-being. A healthy diet supports a strong Flow practice. Think of food as feeding your God vibration.

For food intake, my biggest recommendation is to always notice how you feel after eating certain foods and drinking certain drinks. Pay attention to what you feel before, during, and after. Do you feel well? Do you feel bloated or energetic? Noticing your true response to food after you eat will help you make the right decisions. This means increasing your body awareness. This level of personal awareness will intuitively guide you toward true health and what best serves your body.

Think of food as feeding your God vibration.

In terms of exercise, move your body every day in any way possible. The best way to receive energy from your exercise is to do something you enjoy. This could be walking or running, qigong, yoga, or dance. See if you can get at least twenty minutes of movement in a day. If you're unable to move, try visualization or gentle practices like self-healing. Exercise not only supports your health, but it opens the energy channels. It keeps things moving and flowing. Ensure every part of your body has been moved and you'll keep stress away.

If you can, see to it that every part of your body is touched daily. This keeps the chi flow moving. For example, through self-massage, dry brushing, or tapping. I enjoy "energy massage," which involves working deeper than physical touch and actually moves the chi. Receiving sessions with practitioners like massage therapists is highly recommended. It not only provides increased blood flow to your muscles, but it helps you to release stress and integrate spiritual energy. This includes services such as energy healing and acupuncture, which can be instrumental in integrating higher vibrations. While they may require an investment, these types of sessions can greatly benefit your health.

Sleep is a vital aspect of health. Many people need about seven to nine hours of sleep at night to feel well-rested. It is not just about sleeping but about getting good-quality rest so that you feel awake and fresh in the morning. It isn't uncommon for people to struggle with sleep problems and to feel chronically tired. This is also a reflection of energetic imbalance, of having too much yang energy and not enough yin energy to calm the nervous system. Some people find it hard to turn off their mind at night. It's important to discharge stress and disturbance from your energy system.

The more you work with your chi and practice hands-on healing through Flow meditation, the easier it will be to have restful, nourishing sleep.

I highly recommend exposure to nature as a way for your body to receive positive chi. This helps to open the channels and meridians of the energy body. Nature is instrumental in providing a strong vibration of health. Spending time in nature, especially the practice of earthing — which is simply taking your shoes off and putting your bare feet on the earth — will give you electromagnetic energy (a free energy healing!). Placing your body on the earth or sitting down next to a tree trunk is rejuvenating. You can consciously absorb the positive elements of nature to rebalance and recenter your energy.

PRACTICE:
Meditate on True Health

1. Close your eyes, take a breath, and meditate on the question, "what is true health?" Meditate on this question daily.
2. What is one change you can make today to be healthier?
3. How does health support your Flow practice?

True health is reflected in every part of your life, from your environment, to your relationships, to your work. When you experience balance and support in these areas, you will feel it internally. As your practice develops, your sense of health may intuitively change, and you might find it necessary to make external changes in your life. This may include speaking and expressing your truth so you can live a life that feels aligned to your life intentions.

Learn how to create sacred space for yourself. This is essential to developing any spiritual practice. Keep your home space clear and fresh by removing clutter and dirt. Practice the art of tidying up by donating or throwing away items that do not give you joy. Walk into each room and notice how your energy responds. Your environment subconsciously affects your energy, so be aware of the flow dynamics of your home space (*feng shui*) and do your best to arrange it in a way that allows you to feel inwardly free and uplifted.

Learn how to create sacred space for yourself.

When creating sacred space, it helps to keep a clean, pure, inspiring space for your Flow practice. The energy of the space you meditate in is important. It sets the tone of your meditation. Your sitting space may include flowers, candles, statues, and other items that create a loving feeling and raise the energy in the room. White sage, palo santo smudge sticks, and essential oils are effective clearing tools to release negative energy and create a peaceful environment. It helps to meditate in a secure, contained place where your back is facing a wall and there are no distractions. You might find that it helps to close the door and put your electronic devices outside of the room. Do what you can to make it peaceful.

Learning how to create sacred space is a wonderful way to expand your practice. Sura Flow is a way of practice that promotes true wholeness, health, and compassion. It gives you the resources to thrive in your daily life.

Affirmation: I am attuned to true health.

PART III

THE SURA FLOW
APPROACH TO MEDITATION

*"Those who flow as life flows know
they need no other force."*
— Lao Tzu

CHAPTER 14

WHAT SURA FLOW MEANS

In Sanskrit, *Sura* means divine.

In the 1950s, my mother became an orphan at the young age of eight in South Korea. She was eventually sponsored by a couple in Michigan, named Louise and Ben Donaldson. My mother named me "Louise" after Louise Donaldson, who she wanted me to be like. Grandma Louise dedicated her life to service. She offered music at prisons and sponsored fourteen other orphaned children around the world.

But growing up, I felt very uncomfortable with the name Louise. I knew it wasn't my name. When people called me Louise, it felt off. When I was in my late twenties, I knew I needed to find a new name to live my true self and realize my potential.

For years I had searched for a new name. One day while I was sitting in meditation, I received the inner guidance that my name would be four letters and start with an *S* and end with an *A*. I searched for all combinations of names that fit this convention, but a name still eluded me. About six months later, I was practicing a yoga video that said, *Surya Namaskar* — "sun salutation." In that moment, I saw my name, "Sura."

It wasn't until I took the name Sura that I felt connected to my purpose and potential. It is a word and sound that resonates with me. Changing my name was a personal choice of stepping into my own power and creativity. With changing my first name, I also changed my middle name to Dahn, a Korean word meaning "breath." I wanted my name to represent my intention for this lifetime: "divine breath/flow."

What I know is that we are all God. We are all divine. This name helps me remember that. Sura Flow means "divine flow."

CHAPTER 15

TAPPING INTO THE
POWER OF EFFORTLESS FLOW

Sura Flow is a softer, effortless approach to meditation. It's a basic three-step process that emphasizes relaxation, listening, and intention setting. It's an energy-based practice that empowers you to tap into your creative life force energy, also known as your divine intelligence. We all have access to this chi, the inherent wisdom that lives within us.

Sura Flow is more than a mental, seated practice; it's a whole health system that allows you to live with greater balance, well-being, and harmony with the world around you. The purpose of meditation is liberation. It's the freedom to live as you truly are. Meditation helps you experience self-awareness, which leads to self-realization — knowing who you truly are. It's a practice that gives you the courage to live and express your authentic self.

When you sit in meditation, you have an opportunity to release unconscious blocks and limitations that keep you from being your full self. Meditation offers the opportunity to heal and come into balance. In this peaceful state, you experience effortless flow, a connected, heightened state of being. This flow state connects you to your highest guidance and potential, empowering you to direct the energy of your life from the deepest part of your being.

This state of "being in the zone" is an experience of bliss. Meditation is total immersion. It's complete absorption. You become one with your experience, and in that state, people often lose track of linear time. When you're "in the flow," you feel completely engaged and energized by your experience. Artists and athletes tend to experience "being in the zone" when they are highly connected and performing at peak levels.

Sura Flow is a shift in consciousness.

In this state, you feel a heightened sense of presence, focus, and transcendence. You experience abundance, clarity, and nourishment of your chi. You experience complete oneness. You become existence itself. In the state of flow, your brain changes. It releases neurochemicals including dopamine, serotonin, and endorphins. There is reduced activity in the prefrontal cortex of the brain, and the brain waves begin to slow down to an alpha state (from beta). This indicates that you're in a more relaxed, open state of being.

States of flow affect your performance, your brain, and your energy. It's been shown that these states empower you to feel more energized. There is a natural release and movement of energy when you're in flow state. There's a sense of effortlessness and timelessness. You know when you've experienced a flow state because you feel more alive and awake. Sura Flow is a shift in consciousness. It is a direct experience with the divine.

Flow and Your Higher Intelligence

Your energy is important. Chi is directly connected to your higher self, what some people refer to as universal energy or intuition. Others call it their inner guidance or even their creative genius. It is the divine part of you that is connected to all that is. It's also your spiritual guidance, protecting and guiding you on your true path. It is your wise "God" self, a natural part of who you are. When you're relaxed and at ease, it's easier to sense your chi and hear that small, still whisper that quietly guides you in the right direction.

You could also call this natural energy flow your divine intelligence. In other words, your inner guidance system. It is pure energy consciousness. It is what all things are born of and made from. This includes people, plants, animals, nature, and the world around you. The entire universe is made of energy (chi) and is flowing with consciousness.

You are consciousness. Divine flow, what some people also refer to as "God," is pure energy, pure potential. It is a force of its own.

Chi is a quality of energy. It's a bio-electromagnetic current that runs through your physical body like a superhighway system to keep it running optimally. This chi not only communicates to all the different parts of your body but also to your brain and heart. It has energy information that communicates to you beyond words. The more subtle you become in your awareness through meditation, the more aware you become of energy. You can also listen and pay attention to your energy as a form of guidance.

When you're stressed, you become cut off from the natural flow of energy. Stress is chi that is blocked. It accumulates into tension. It blocks your energy flow. When you're stressed, it puts you into survival mode, which activates fear. This tends to disconnect you from higher states of being, such as peace and inspiration. When you're experiencing the fear state, you cannot experience love, and vice versa.

Stress, fear, and anxiety go hand-in-hand. You can experience a fear-based state, a neutral state, or an open, loving state. You have the power to shift your own focus. This ability becomes more accessible through consistent practice. By refocusing your attention, you can direct your awareness to your body and breath. This simple practice connects you to your inherent life force energy. Breath and body awareness empowers you to experience more freedom and expression in your everyday life.

When you tap into a deeper place within yourself through stillness, your actions, words, and intentions develop power. They arise from a more aware, connected place, a place of pure presence. In meditation, you get in touch with your energy — a more instinctive place within your being. Your actions become spontaneous and free, less calculating and controlling. There is less thinking and more being. You'll find yourself taking action instead of talking. Your life becomes a meditation in motion.

It's about tapping into the deeper, instinctive place within you.

A dedicated practice is not about following rules or adhering to any sense of rigid form or doctrine; it's about discovering what true healing and peace mean to you. Your practice is about learning how to tap into the state of Zen on your own and how to sustain inner states that truly serve your health and well-being.

Through Sura Flow, you develop fluidity in the moment so you know how to remain flexible and open. You learn how to be fresh in the moment. When you're tuned in, you become decisive. It's about tapping into the deeper, instinctive place within you. When you tap into your own energy, you are free to respond with skillfulness and grace. You are free to become your unique self.

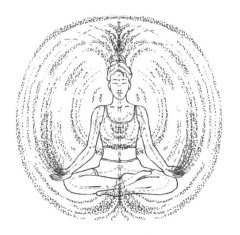

Sura Flow Meditation

Sura Flow is a tool to raise your consciousness. When you raise your consciousness, you improve the quality of energy you experience throughout your life. Health is energy. It has a resonance. It also has a vibration. Through the practice of Flow meditation, you find yourself becoming naturally more healthy.

The energy of health directly impacts the quality of your life and chi. Your life force energy is precious. When your chi is balanced, through good diet, exercise, and enough rest, all aspects of your life align naturally and come into greater balance; your health, relationships, work, and sense of purpose harmonize.

You can tell when your chi is bright. You feel fresh — enlivened. There's pep in your step and a spark in your eye. There's a feeling of positivity within you. Health emanates through your skin. You might notice a radiant glow when your energy is flowing. When your chi is low, your mood is low, and you may experience depression or anxiety. Your chi or energy may seem grey or cloudy. Flow practice helps clear your energy so you feel balanced and energetic. It also helps you cultivate beauty.

When you're connected to your life force energy, you notice it in both your inner and outer experiences. You feel a greater sense of confidence and daily calm. You become fully engaged in all aspects of your life, whether they are good or bad. You are less affected by the bad things that happen because you're more grounded in your sense of self. It becomes easier to stop taking things personally. Without getting stuck on the small stuff, life takes on a new dimension that is full of possibilities.

CHAPTER 16

THREE STEPS TO THE SURA FLOW APPROACH

Sura Flow is a softer approach to meditation that invites healing, inner guidance, and energy cultivation. Our natural state of being is peace. The Sura Flow practice teaches you how to be truly present in the moment while responding to life's events with ease and skillfulness.

Before Getting Started

First and foremost, it's vital to remember self-compassion when you're developing your Flow practice. Too often, people are hard on themselves in all aspects of their lives. They berate and judge themselves unnecessarily. Meditation is no exception. It's natural to try too hard and even force a meditative mindset in the beginning. But that can turn into a struggle. This approach can easily lead to frustration and, in some cases, anxiety.

Compassion is the anchor for a long-lasting, sustainable Flow practice. It's important to have patience and not expect results right away. It's natural to have erratic experiences during your seated sessions. You might have a good, peaceful practice one day and feel like you're flailing the next. Every "sit" is different. As much as you may want to, you cannot reproduce positive experiences. Every experience is unique. Through compassion and self-love you can deepen into your practice.

Compassion is the anchor for a long-lasting sustainable Flow practice.

Sura Flow provides a profound opportunity to heal. Healing is the process of becoming whole. The Merriam-Webster dictionary defines healing as "the process of making [someone] or becoming sound or healthy again." Healing allows you to return to your center. It gives you the energy just "to be" and express your true self.

Healing is a natural part of evolution. When you allow yourself to move beyond the mental construct of meditation, you get deeply connected to your body's wisdom. You tap into the natural intelligence that flows through you and you heal. It gives you the opportunity to see and experience life from a renewed perspective. You become open to your divine insights and find the resolve to release old wounds that have kept you stuck.

One of the greatest benefits you can receive from Sura Flow is emotional healing. When you allow yourself to get in touch with your deeper, darker emotions, letting yourself truly feel what you're feeling inside, you become more centered and grounded. Notice how you feel after a good cry. There's often a sense of catharsis and with that a feeling of relief. It brings a deeper sense of power and embodiment.

When you repress your emotions, you repress your energy. You keep yourself from your authentic power and who you truly are. Many of us are afraid to feel bad feelings and really be alone with our thoughts. This is why people stay constantly busy and distracted, avoiding the uncomfortable feelings they truly feel inside. It only promotes that sense of emptiness, desperation, or anxiety. Anxiety is often a symptom of repressing deeper emotions. It's a sign of resistance. It's the body's way of communicating that something is out of balance.

When you feel stressed or anxious, that's a signal to stop and pay attention. Say the truth of what you feel in that moment. Expressing truth is healing. For example, simply saying to yourself, "I feel scared," is a step in the right direction. This allows you to connect back to yourself. When you acknowledge your own true experience, it automatically begins to release pent-up energy. This is the opportunity that Flow practice has to offer: balancing your emotions and raising your own emotional awareness.

Expressing truth is healing.

When you find yourself having challenging emotions, remember to invite in the energy of compassion. It is through loving kindness that you can find the strength to move through any challenges that arise during your practice. With compassionate awareness, anything becomes possible.

When to Meditate

The best time to practice is first thing in the morning. In the morning, your mind is still relatively calm from sleep. You haven't yet engaged in the busyness of your day. Most of the world is still in a state of calm. You can take advantage of that time by absorbing the peace of your morning. You'll find that starting your day centered and clear has a positive effect on the rest of your day.

Do your best to meditate every day. It helps you develop your practice and get into a flow. If you don't have a lot of time, consider meditating for a few minutes every day rather than for a big chunk of time at once in the middle of the week. The key is to make your practice consistent. Make it a healthy habit, just like brushing your teeth or taking a shower; you don't think about whether to do it, you just do. You do it to maintain a level of health and hygiene.

The same goes for your practice. It's a time to cleanse and reset; to release old energy and stress and start afresh. It's a sacred time for yourself. It's a divine appointment. Set a time each day when you'll commit to your practice, even if it's just five minutes. It's a time for your own spiritual growth. You'll find that having a routine is paramount to receiving the full benefit of your Flow practice.

Three Basic Steps to the Sura Flow Approach

In the Sura Flow approach, you practice three basic steps. The first step is relaxation. The second step is awareness listening. And the final step is intention.

Sura Flow

Step 1: Relax - start by letting go
Step 2: Listen - be receptive to your experience
Step 3: Intend - apply the energy of your meditation

You begin your Sura Flow practice with relaxation to bring about a sense of ease. It also releases tension and opens the energy channels of the body. Relaxation invites receptivity and moves you to the second stage of your practice: heart listening.

In heart listening, you're allowing all to arise in your awareness without resistance. You're simply paying attention. You're aware with the intention of listening from your heart. Listening puts you into a deeper state of receptivity where you can notice and receive messages from your divine consciousness.

As you cultivate energy and stillness throughout your practice, you can harness this energy and direct it with your intention, applying this at the beginning and end of your Flow practice. In this way, you harness the energy from your practice. You can apply your intention toward blessings, healing, or even a heartfelt desire you want to manifest.

Contemplating an intention in your heart while in a peaceful state allows it to enter your consciousness more deeply. When you are in a state of non-resistance, your intention manifests readily. When you are in a state of pure peace, you become receptive to shifting and moving energy. You'll discover that the more you meditate, the more potent your intentions become.

CHAPTER 17

RELAXATION

*"Everything can be done better
from a place of relaxation."*
— **Stephen C. Paul**

The key to Flow practice is relaxation. When you
release your physical, emotional, and mental tension,
you allow your life force energy to flow.

If you have a lot of energy, it may mean that you
need actual physically demanding exercise to help
you relax. I suggest burning it off before you sit to
meditate. You can exercise, dance, run, do yoga. Do
what you need to do to let go of the angst and disturbance in your body before you practice. You'll find
that it's best to release tension and cultivate relaxation
before you enter the state of meditation.

Your state of being affects the quality of your
practice. When you have a lot of tension and anxiety,
you will find it harder to be still. You're likely to feel
agitated, which may even become magnified the
more you continue to sit. This is why some people
find meditation disturbing — because they have not
taken time to prepare for stillness.

159

Through meditation, you open the flow channels of your body. You create an optimal inner environment that is ready for stillness.

When you are relaxed, it's easier to focus and be present.

During the Sura Flow practice, as you start with relaxation, it's also a time of "setting the energy" of your practice. Begin with a sense of sacred space and connection. To experience effortless flow in any endeavor, whether a sitting practice or in life, it helps to start with the intention of relaxation. When you are relaxed, it's easier to focus and be present. It allows you to receive greater benefit from your practice. Relaxation helps everything flow better in your life.

Why Relaxation Is Important

Many people live in a constant state of stress, also known as the "fight or flight" mode. This mode can include anything from a mild state of stress to full-blown anxiety. It's often marked by tension, shallow breathing, and a frenetic mind.

When you are in this stress state, you are connected to the part of your mind I refer to as "stress brain."

This is the part of the brain that's constantly thinking and running at 100 mph. When you're in this part of your brain, it can feel impossible to slow down your thoughts. Intense activity in the prefrontal area of the brain is often marked by the beta brain wave state. Beta brain wave states are the fastest brain waves of low amplitude that include active, engaged mental activity.

Relaxation Initiates a Healing Response

Sura Flow begins with relaxation because it shifts you from thinking to being.

When you consciously shift from the stress response (the sympathetic nervous system) to the relaxation response, your body and brain begin a different process. It activates the parasympathetic nervous system, which allows you to "rest and digest." Your body begins to release chemicals that allow your organs to slow down, which in turn increases blood flow to the brain. Your breath rate slows down, your heart rate lowers, and your muscles begin to relax. Your blood pressure lowers, and your digestive system and hormones return to balance.

It's possible to slow down your mental activity by making the *intention* to relax your mind. When you prepare for your meditation practice, simply close your eyes and intend to relax your body and your mind. As you consciously begin to pay attention to your breath, it will slow down. This sends a message to your brain and your body that it's safe to let go.

As you listen to your breath with heightened levels of presence, you might notice that it naturally begins to shift and deepen. As you slow down your breath, it initiates the relaxation response, a natural healing state for your body and mind. This tells your body that it's safe to eliminate toxins and begin a regenerative process. By engaging the parasympathetic nervous system, you return to the state of homeostasis.

Relaxation leads to stillness and surrender.

Neuroscience writer Nicoletta Lanese defines homeostasis as "the ability to maintain a relatively stable internal state that persists despite changes in the world outside. All living organisms, from plants to puppies to people, must regulate their internal environment to process energy and ultimately survive."

You can learn how to self-regulate your internal state through the practice of relaxation. The process of homeostasis supports your health system. The World Health Organization describes health as complete emotional, social, and physical well-being — not just being free from illness and disease. Being in a physiological state of relaxation is vital for maintaining true health and longevity. The conscious practice of relaxation shifts you mentally, physically, and emotionally. It prepares you for meditation. Think of relaxation as stretching before a dance performance to help prepare the body for physical endurance. You can slip into the state of meditation naturally by learning how to let go and release tension first. With relaxation, you can learn to develop resilience and self-regulation of your thoughts, emotions, and breath.

Relaxation is an essential skill to develop for meditation. It helps you to become receptive and allows you to enter the state of meditation effortlessly. Relaxation leads to stillness and surrender, two essential inner states that help deepen your personal meditation practice.

The Purpose of Relaxation

In relaxation, you're taking a proactive step by setting the energy of your meditation. Think of it as preparing your inner room. When you meditate, would you prefer to sit in a clean room or a messy, chaotic one? Of course, most of us would choose to sit in a clean, serene space. The same holds true for the inner space you cultivate for Flow practice.

If your inner space is chaotic and noisy, it will be harder to concentrate and feel calm. If your inner space is open, relaxed, and free, it will be easier to sit. You'll feel more receptive and receive the calming benefit of meditation practice. By tending to your inner sanctuary, you set the energy of your meditation practice so it's easier to experience the higher states of being such as peace.

You can practice relaxation as long as needed to prepare for your awareness listening practice. This may take anywhere from five to twenty minutes. In the beginning, it may serve you to only practice relaxation. If you're just starting out in meditation, I highly recommend twenty-one days of relaxation practice first. It's okay to only have a personal practice of relaxation if that serves you best. Relaxation is a very effective practice that anyone can benefit from.

You will notice that the more you practice relaxation, the easier it is to let go and relax throughout the day. Each time you practice, you fall into the state of relaxation more easily. It becomes more accessible to you, and you are able to command it at will.

When you learn to self-regulate your internal state, you regulate your own breath rate, your body's biorhythms, and your emotions. By learning how to anchor yourself in your breath and making the intention to open yourself to your energy, you'll see that it gets easier to shift from 100 mph to 20 mph. With time, you'll find yourself gaining mastery over your inner self through relaxation.

There are several ways to set the energy of relaxation and peace before your practice. Some of these practices are well-suited for experienced practitioners who understand energy cultivation and healing; however, anyone can learn how to heal themselves through meditation.

Practice: The Body Scan

A body scan is the practice of scanning your awareness through all parts of your body. This promotes relaxation and presence in your physical body. It also helps you cultivate embodiment by inviting your energy flow throughout your whole body.

During a body scan, you're paying attention to the various parts of your physical body, as well as their sensations. This helps you to develop body awareness. During a body scan practice, you bring your attention from your head space into your body space, and you can begin to experience a heightened sense of presence.

Body scan meditation allows you to develop greater awareness of your physical body. Paying attention to the nuances and sensations of your body heightens your own individual awareness. You'll notice that a thought, sensation, or emotion elicits a body response such as tension or relaxation. Having an awareness of this response and receiving real-time feedback empowers you to make a shift to anchor yourself into a more stable inner state.

A body scan practice also helps to relax the monkey mind. By shifting your attention to your body and becoming aware of your whole physical body, you allow your body to relax. This process helps you become more present. By anchoring your awareness in your body, you will experience a sense of ease and peace that sets you up for your Flow practice.

Begin a body scan by resting your attention at your feet and gently moving your awareness up through each part of your physical body. This moves you from the farthest point from your head, the busiest place in your body!

You can practice relaxation lying down, sitting in a chair with both your feet firmly planted on the floor, or in an easy seated pose with the legs crossed. Lying down allows you to fully relax. However, if you lie down, be mindful that you do not fall asleep. Do your best to stay alert and awake.

Body Scan Guided Sequence

As you scan your body, simply bring your attention to that part of your body.

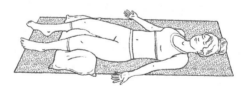

Relax Lying Down

Slowly repeat each body part in your head starting from your feet and moving to your ankles, lower legs, knees, upper legs, hips, buttocks, groin, belly, back, chest, shoulder, arms, fingers, upper chest, neck, back of the head, head, face, scalp, brain, eyes, nose, jaw, inner organs, heart and bones, joints and spine. Simply follow the natural map of your body and work your way from the bottoms of your feet up to the whole head.

In body scan meditation, you can also imagine the Earth's magnetic chi flowing up through the soles of your feet and into your body. As the Earth's energy flows, allow yourself to release tension, toxins, and stress. You can envision and intend this.

See the Earth's energy nourishing all the cells of your body, your muscles, tendons, and inner organs, filling you up from the inside out. Let its energy cleanse and rejuvenate all parts of your body and your energy field. Allow yourself to feel complete resonance with the Earth and notice its calming effect.

Practice: Energy Scan

You are more than your physical body. You have an energy field that surrounds you like a bubble. It's called an aura. This is the area that includes your personal space. Your aura is a natural boundary around your energy field. It extends about twelve to twenty-four inches around your physical body. For example, you can feel it when someone enters your personal space because they have entered your auric space.

Your auric field contains your thoughts, moods, emotions, and consciousness. It's what people describe as your "vibe." You can instantly receive a strong sense of a person by looking at their auric field. For example, you can get an easy first impression by sensing if a person has "positive" or "negative" vibes.

When the field of your aura becomes disrupted, you will often feel scattered, diffused, and dissipated. It's much harder to be present and focused. You may also notice that your energy responds to being in certain places and environments. You might feel refreshed being outside in nature or feel drained at a busy shopping mall. Your energy is affected by everything within and around you. This includes your thoughts, your emotions, your environment, the people around you, and your work.

Your aura reflects your state of being. When your aura is balanced, full, and flowing, you feel present and buoyant. When your energy is heavy, your aura will reflect that density. When this happens, you're likely to feel lower emotional states such as fear and stress. The key to finding true well-being is to become aware of your energy and let it work *for you* during meditation.

Similar to the practice of qigong or tai chi, the intention of an energy scan is to move energy (chi) throughout your energy body. By becoming aware of your energy and learning how to balance it, you develop a stronger sense of presence and vitality. This practice helps you stay energetically and physically fresh.

In a self-healing energy scan, you start by becoming aware of your own energy. When you become aware of your physical and energetic state, you become empowered to shift it.

Start with this question: *how does your energy feel?*

If you were to envision your energy like a sphere around your body, does it seem whole, balanced, and full, or does it feel chaotic, holey, and unbalanced?

Gently scan your energy from the top of your head all the way down around you, into your feet and into the Earth. Become aware of your spheric field above your head and below your feet. Where do you sense most of your energy? Is it congregated toward your head and shoulders? Do you have energy awareness in your legs and feet?

You have an incredible energy system you can tap into through spiritual practice.

With energy healing, you start by making the intention to balance and move your energy. Imagine that your energy is flowing throughout your body into your aura, connected to the Earth below and the heavens above. Feel your divine connection to all that is.

Practice: Sensing Chi

Rub the palms of your hands together. Do this for at least sixty seconds. Rub vigorously. After a minute, let yourself gently pull your hands apart, keeping them close together (about an inch or two apart). Notice if you feel a magnetism or pull between your hands. You may feel warmth or tingling between the palms of your hands. This is your *prana*, your life force energy.

When you are healthy, this bio-electromagnetic force is strong. You are radiant and full of energy. When this magnetism slows down or becomes stagnant or stuck, you have weak chi. You will notice this shift in your energy and your mood. You're likely to feel less energetic, stagnant, and unmotivated when your chi is low.

Balance Your Energy

Energy runs through your body like electricity. When that electric current gets blocked, you're more likely to experience pain, blocks, and inner tension. You may even look dull or weak. This is why stress can be so draining: it lowers your chi. You have an incredible energy system you can tap into through spiritual practice. When you learn how to manage your energy, you can also learn how to skillfully manage your stress and health.

Balance Your Energy

Self-healing starts with your intention to clear, ground, and collect your energy. You may notice that you feel more contained at the beginning of the day, but gradually you feel less focused and "together." This is because your energy naturally dissipates throughout the day. As you engage in more activities and interact with others, you can lose the potency of your chi. When your attention is moving in many different directions, it also diffuses your life force energy.

The key to balancing your energy is to tune in to your own energy (spirit) and allow it to be present in your physical body. You will feel more centered and energetic from learning how to ground and balance your own chi.

Practice: Self-Aura Healing

Take your hands and rub them together. Feel the magnetism between your palms to help increase your sensitivity and awareness to energy. Gently sweep your aura and your energy body with your hands. This includes the area that extends out about one to two feet beyond your physical body. With your intention and awareness, feel the energy around you and make the intention to cleanse and clear it.

You may notice hot areas, sticky spots, or cooler, more empty areas. Simply be aware of them and make the intention to smooth out and balance your energy field. Imagine releasing any dense or foreign energy into the Earth's molten core, where it can be transmuted. Notice what you feel and sense where you're clearing and releasing old energy.

Self-Aura Healing

Some people can feel the effect of a self-healing auric cleanse. Others may not, and that's perfectly okay. If you don't feel anything, then simply work with the intention to let go and release old energy. It takes time to develop the awareness of energy. What is most important is your intention. Continue practicing if you feel a benefit to your sense of well-being. During a self-energy cleanse, you may notice subtle shifts including a greater sense of calm, presence, and clarity.

Now that you have released old, stagnant energy, be sure to refill yourself with positive energy. At the end of your energy clearing, gather your energy back like a golden sun above your crown. Bring your energy into present time from all the people, places, and spaces where you might have left your energy. Call it back with love. Gather it from the past and future and energize your golden sun like a magnet. Envision it fully charged and radiant.

Gathering Golden Suns

The golden sun is your life force essence. After reclaiming your energy and power, gently invite this beautiful golden light into the top of your head, through your center line, into your entire body, and out into your auric field. Imagine that you are sitting in a radiant orb of your own energy and gently ground it to the Earth. Make the intention to seal and protect your energy field.

If there are any places you feel that your auric field is not strong, then continue energy work in those areas. Imagine filling in the areas that feel empty or weak in and around your body. See those areas become nourished with warm, liquid, golden light. Complete your healing by envisioning and sealing a circle of golden light around your physical body.

Practice: Hands-On Healing

In addition to aura cleansing, you can practice hands-on self-healing. This is a very effective way to receive more prana and energy into your physical body before meditation. Your hands have an energy center located at your palms. Energy flows through your hands. You can sense this energy by rubbing your hands together as we did in the previous section. This helps to get the energy moving.

Have you ever noticed that when you're hurt or in pain, you intuitively place your hand on an injury? Your hands have healing power. They transmit energy. Think of your hands as circuits that you place on your body to regenerate positive energy within you.

By doing so, you allow the flow of energy to go back into your body to restore and boost your chi.

You can practice any intuitive hand placement on your own body.

> ## The four hand placements I recommend for self-healing are:
>
> 1. Hands on heart. Gently place both hands on your heart center.
> 2. Hands on dan tien. In Chinese medicine, the dan tien, loosely translated as "elixir chi," is located two inches below the belly button. This is a place where you store energy and power.
> 3. Belly and heart. Place one hand on your belly (solar plexus), one on your heart.
> 4. Dan tien and heart. Place one hand on your dan tien and one hand on your heart.

Hands-On Healing

Before you practice energy healing, send yourself the intention of unconditional love. This simple practice will get your chi flowing. Love is pure energy flow. Gently place your hands on your desired area of your body. You will feel instinctively "pulled" to place your hands where they will be of most benefit. Trust where your hands are being guided.

First, allow yourself to relax and become receptive. Imagine universal energy flowing effortlessly from your hands into your body. Allow yourself to relax and receive. Let yourself enjoy the experience and receive the pleasure of subtle energy movement in your physical body.

If you like, you can say positive affirmations such as "infinite blessings" or "unconditional love." A wonderful affirmation to practice in places of tension is "I feel safe here." You can also include short prayers of intention such as "thank you for sending blessings." Notice how the energy flows when you gently focus your attention on your positive affirmations.

Become aware of your true experience and notice any shifts as you practice hands-on healing. It helps if you can have skin-to-skin contact, but it's still effective if you're providing hands-on healing through your clothes. You may notice energy in your hands, warmth, or even tingling. You may notice a flow of energy moving through your hands and into your body. Let yourself be open. Be aware of how you feel during a self-healing session and how you feel afterward.

Practice: Grounding and Golden Suns

When you are grounded, you feel secure and present. You can do this by connecting to the energy of the Earth. When you're not grounded, you're likely to feel restless and uneasy. You may also feel spacey, floaty, or out of your body. When you're ungrounded, it's hard to feel centered or make any real progress.

Grounding gives you a neutral place to land your energy. When you're stressed, it's because you're focusing your attention on a stressful thought, person, or experience. You might notice how anxious you feel after you talk to someone with anxiety. It's because you've focused your attention on that person instead of staying grounded in your own energy.

When you're unconsciously connecting to energy that's around you, it's easy to feel scattered and off-center. Also, the more exposed you are to chaotic energy, the more likely you are to have stress and energy that accumulate in your physical body and nervous system.

If you haven't taken time to consciously "discharge" this frenetic energy, it can build in your body and ultimately take a toll as chronic stress. This is when people experience frayed nerves and become easily irritated. It's from a build-up of negative psychic energy. Because of this, you may suffer from chronic stress or insomnia or just feel "off."

Learning how to manage stress is about learning how to shift your focus. When you're grounded, you feel stable and connected. Grounding is an anchor that allows you to become centered. It also allows you to release any pent-up foreign or stressful energy and flow it back into the Earth, giving you an opportunity to let go and return to a neutral balance.

With grounding, you can also practice bringing the Earth's energy back into your own body to feel nourished and rejuvenated. Have you ever noticed how good you feel when you put your body right on the earth or walk barefoot on the beach? That's because you're picking up the electromagnetic energy of the Earth. It provides a natural healing effect. "Earthing" allows you to release toxins and connect to the vibration of the Earth's energy.

> *Grounding is an anchor that allows you to become centered.*

When you resonate with the stability of the Earth, you become centered and connected. Grounding helps you feel secure. It naturally shields you from frenetic energy around you. Grounding provides you energetic protection. It gives you a resource to tap into to flow your chi. With deep energetic roots into the Earth, you can branch out and expand your potential.

Grounding Guided Sequence

Bring all of your attention into your whole body and into your feet. Imagine that you have a grounding cord, like a big tree trunk, that extends from your body down into the center of the Earth. Envision the roots wrapping around the core of the Earth at least three times. Let your connection to the Earth's core be effortless. The moment you intend to imagine it, it happens. Notice how it feels to be centered and grounded to the center of the Earth.

Grounded and Flowing

With your intention and visualization, imagine releasing any old energy into the Earth's core, where it can be transmuted and transformed by the molten lava there. Release all your problems, tension, stress, and past and future events into the Earth. Let go of other people's energy, problems, and thoughts.

See all the energy that doesn't serve you flow down easily and effortlessly through the grounding cord. Release all your responsibilities, to-do lists, and any foreign energy that doesn't belong to you. You can let go of your work and any past experiences that may be bothering you. Notice where you feel a sense of release happening in your physical body and energy field.

Empty out all stress and tension through your grounding cord. Pay attention to how you feel internally when you release any old or stagnant energy. When you feel empty and clear, call back all of your vital essence in the form of a golden sun above your crown. Allow it to descend into your center and fill your body up with your own pure energy.

For more details, see the practice described in "Self Chi-bath." You can also visit: *suraflow.org/practices* for guided video instructions on all the energy practices.

Practice: Invocation and Prayer

You can set the energy of your practice by raising your own energy. When you start with spiritual resources that you connect to, you invite the quality of that energy into your practice.

Everyone's spiritual resource is different. It can be anything: God, nature, a higher power, your divine guides. It's the representation of your highest divine consciousness that invites a feeling of peace, love, and gratitude. This sets the sacred space of your practice.

You can simply imagine these resources or call upon them in your mind's eye. "God, divine love, angels."

Pay attention when you practice this individually or in a group. You may notice a shift in your state of being when you invoke your spiritual resources.

This is your practice; you can connect to anything that brings about a feeling of love. By invoking your spiritual allies, and the feeling of blessings and gratitude, you'll notice that focusing your attention on the energy that inspires you will shift you into a higher state. This empowers you to drop in and feel safe to open yourself to receiving positive universal energy.

Preparing for Your Sitting Meditation

You can meditate in any position, but the three most common are sitting cross-legged, sitting in a chair, and lying down. The most important thing is that you feel comfortable and at ease when you're meditating.

If you have the flexibility to sit on the floor in an easy, cross-legged position, that is ideal. It helps to have a meditation cushion or thick pillow to place underneath your sitz bones (the pelvic bones that bear weight when you are seated). Let the pillow prop up your sitz bones so that your knees fall slightly below your hips. This creates a tripod effect that allows you to sit more easily with a straight spine.

Many people do not have the flexibility to sit cross-legged on the floor. That's perfectly okay. The next best option then is to sit in a chair during your meditation. If you're sitting in a chair, I recommend sitting away from the back of the chair so your spine is straight and both your feet are firmly planted on the floor. If your feet do not reach the floor, place blocks or books under your feet so they have direct contact with the floor.

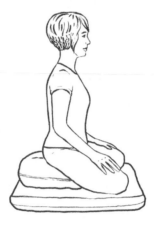

Aligned Seated Position

Be sure to sit with a straight spine. Your spine should be tall and free with the feeling of your head balancing perfectly on top of your spine. Relax your whole body and let your shoulders fall down your back. You can sit with your hands resting palms down on your upper thighs, which helps create a sense of grounding. You can also rest the back of your hands on your thighs with your palms facing upward to receive energy. You can clasp your hands or choose a healing hand-hold by placing your hands on your lower belly.

If you're physically unable to sit comfortably, you can also lie down for your meditation practice. Not everyone has the physical ability to sustain a seated position. Lying down creates a different meditative effect; however, it is just as viable for people who are unable to sit. You can lie down on a yoga mat on the floor with a pillow underneath your knees for back support. Be mindful not to fall asleep and stay as alert as possible during your meditation.

You can meditate with eyes closed or gently open. If they are open, keep a soft inward gaze at one point, such as the tip of your nose or a candle flame. The eye gaze is soft and relaxed, so you are receiving a visual image in front of you. Keeping an open-eye gaze helps you stay grounded in the present moment.

Alternatively, you can close your eyes. I find this position more comfortable, allowing me to go deeper into a state of meditation. However, even with eyes closed, see if you can keep the intention to stay present in your body during your meditation.

You can breathe in and out of your nose during meditation. You can also breathe in through the nose and out through the mouth for cleansing breaths. The key is to pay attention to your breath. The breathing method I recommend is this subtle awareness of slow breathing, pausing between each in breath and each outbreath. Pause and find a moment of stillness between each and every breath.

Your breath is your most vital connection to chi. By constantly paying attention to your breath in your Sura Flow practice and throughout your day, you cultivate longevity. Your practice raises awareness of your breath and *how* you breathe. By having a constant awareness of your body and breath, you develop continual self-awareness in the moment. These simple practices raise your consciousness.

CHAPTER 18

HEART LISTENING

"The best and most beautiful things
in this world cannot be seen
nor even touched, but just
felt in the heart."
— Helen Keller

Heart listening practice is the practice of awareness listening, also known as "heart awareness." The practice of awareness requires no specific technique. Traditionally, people gently follow their breath as an anchor. In the practice of heart awareness, your primary focus is the heart center. You allow all that you're experiencing to rise to the surface of your experience. You become aware of this through the intention of compassionate awareness.

In heart listening practice, there is no concentration or forceful effort to try to make your experience different. There is no judgment or suppression. During awareness practice, you simply observe and pay attention to your true experience. You fully allow your own experience. This includes all your thoughts, feelings, sensations, and emotions. You may have a thought bubble up continually, and in this practice, you simply observe the thought without attachment or resistance.

This approach is very similar to awareness or insight meditation. However, in this practice, you actively engage the heart and listen with compassion. By practicing presence together with heart-centered listening, you also become receptive to the insights and guidance from your own inherent wisdom. You open yourself to the divine guidance that flows from your own heart.

Move Beyond the Mind in Meditation Practice

Oftentimes, when people practice meditation, they feel overwhelmed by the racing thoughts in their mind. They sit for twenty minutes and feel that all they have done in that time is sit with their own chaotic thoughts.

When people meditate, they tend to focus their attention in their mind. It's natural to place attention here, but this can be a challenging space to navigate. The mind is often in a perpetual state of flux. The "monkey mind" is constantly jumping from here to there.

In meditation practice, it can be difficult to make real progress when your primary attention is focused in your head. You may notice that it tends to feel more compressed and less spacious when you focus your attention there.

For a moment, close your eyes and notice "where" you tend to "be" in your brain. You might notice that your attention is primarily in the front part of your brain, near your forehead. When you're constantly thinking, you're inhabiting a part of your brain that is mostly in the frontal lobe.

The prefrontal cortex (located behind your eyes and forehead) is the part of your brain where you're constantly assessing situations and engaging in past and future thinking. This is a very busy part of your mind. It's where executive functions happen, including the ability to know between good and bad, expectations, and social discernment. When your attention is focused here, it can be a difficult place to try and remain calm. There are other places where you can focus your attention in meditation that can provide more calm and clarity.

The Heart's Intelligence

The heart has a vast intelligence system you can tap into through the practice of meditation. It's a place to receive deeper wisdom, perspective, and intuition. When you focus your attention on your heart during meditation, you will notice a different experience, one that feels more connected, present, and compassionate.

In addition to a vast intelligence system, the heart contains the most powerful electromagnetic energy (chi) in the human body. The heart emits 100 times more energy than the electromagnetic field of the human brain. It is a powerful generator of energy that is vital to your health and well-being. Your heart communicates on a level of energy that your brain cannot. It is the vehicle through which you express love, empathy, and emotions.

The HeartMath Institute, a leading meditation organization that provides biofeedback tools and applications to promote heart coherence, has done extensive research on the intelligence of the heart. Neurocardiologist Dr. J. Andrew Armour discovered there is a "brain in the heart." He observed that "the heart possessed a complex and intrinsic nervous system that is a brain."

> When you focus
> your attention on
> your heart during
> meditation, you will notice
> a different experience,
> one that feels more
> connected, present, and
> compassionate.

The scientists at the HeartMath Institute have found that the heart is the source of emotional intelligence and governs our ability to manage our emotions.

A 2012 article states, *"From our research at the HeartMath Institute, we've concluded that intelligence and intuition are heightened when we learn to listen more deeply to our own heart. It's through learning how to decipher messages we receive from our heart that we gain the keen perception needed to effectively manage our emotions in the midst of life's challenges. The more we learn to listen to and follow our heart intelligence, the more educated, balanced, and coherent our emotions become. Without the guiding influence of the heart we easily fall prey to reactive emotions such as insecurity, anger, fear, and blame as well as other energy-draining reactions and behaviors."*

The heart knows. It has guidance and information the mind alone cannot access. It provides a higher perspective. This perspective empowers you to experience a greater sense of peace and empathy. In the Sura Flow practice, you focus on centering and listening from your heart center. This helps to cultivate connection with your heart's intelligence. Heart-centered attention promotes flow and expanded awareness.

The heart knows.

The Power of the Heart

Preparing for Your Heart Listening Practice

You can practice awareness listening sitting comfortably, either cross- legged or in a chair. If you're unable to sit, you can also lie down on your back. Adjust yourself so that you are completely comfortable. Sit with your spine straight and ensure that your neck, shoulders, and back are tension-free. Do your best to be still during your practice, but listen to your body if you need to make adjustments.

It's important you feel good and comfortable. You can move and stretch until you feel open and relaxed in your seated position. You do not need to endure intense pain during a meditation session. However, it's good to pause whenever you feel the need to move. It can be an itch or your legs starting to go numb. Observe the sensation without the label, and be with it.

If you find yourself in pain, do your best to move in a way that does not distract you from your practice. It's possible to adjust your position in a way that allows you to stay connected to your meditation.

When you begin awareness listening, start by becoming relaxed and centered. Let yourself feel your connection to the Earth. Being grounded and centered opens you to your divine consciousness. It also helps you experience heightened levels of presence.

Train Yourself to Be Compassionate

During any meditation practice, it's important to be aware of *how* you're focusing your attention. Notice where your attention goes when you sit for meditation. Take some time and shift your attention to different places in and around your body. Notice what helps you feel most present and alert. Where do you enjoy resting your attention?

When you're centered, it's easier to be present. In Sura Flow, maintain a gentle focus on the heart center. Stay inwardly connected by shifting your attention from the mind to the heart. It will help you feel more expanded and in tune with your divine consciousness.

By focusing your awareness on your heart space, you may notice you experience a heightened state of compassion. It also helps to quiet the mind when your attention is focused in your heart center. Compassion is the seat of awareness listening. When you develop the skill of compassion, you experience less stress and self-judgment. This is often the source of tension: a harsh mindset. When you have negative thoughts about yourself or others, compassion helps to dispel those thoughts. Self-empathy cultivates resilience and understanding. It also helps you shift the quality of your thoughts with less effort.

The practice of compassion empowers you to extend loving kindness toward yourself and others. It is easy to get into a negative space with meditation and even berate yourself while you're sitting. It's not uncommon to start thinking, "I'm bad at meditation" or "I'm not good enough." This kind of mindset is discouraging and only slows down your progress. It's important to cultivate an encouraging tone toward yourself.

Compassion is the seat of awareness listening.

When you experience compassion toward yourself and others, you'll discover a superpower that allows you to move effortlessly through life with less judgment and fear. This kind of self-care promotes flow in all aspects of your life. When you're kinder to yourself, life gets easier. When you practice, it helps to start with self-compassion because when you're kind toward yourself, it's easier to be kind toward others.

In Sura Flow, begin with the intention of compassion. Self-compassion is the nourishment that helps your practice to take root and flower. The practice of loving kindness will take you far, not only in your meditation practice but in life. It enhances your internal state, your thoughts, and your health. Think of loving kindness as fertilizer for your practice. The practice of compassion will help you grow.

Meditating With Hands-On Healing

The Practice of Heart Listening

In awareness listening, you become aware of all that's arising while maintaining a steady, gentle focus on the heart center. This allows you to observe from a more neutral, compassionate space while staying centered and present in your physical body. If thoughts arise, see them come and go like clouds in the sky. You don't have to resist them or engage them, just watch them go by. See if you can be an observer in your practice.

Opening to a witness perspective and observing without judgment provides a level of neutrality and detachment in your inner process. In awareness listening, you listen with a sense of compassion to all that's arising in the present moment.

Practice: Heart Breaths

To begin your heart listening practice, start with three simple heart breaths. This helps you connect to the energy of your heart and anchor your awareness there. If you like, you can place a hand on your heart so you can connect more readily to the energy of your heart.

Begin your heart breaths by inhaling from the backside of the heart, then exhaling through the front of your heart. Pause between every in-breath and out-breath. With each breath, allow the center of your heart to soften and open. This allows your heart center to feel flowing and spacious.

When you're taking your heart breaths, allow yourself to consciously slow down. Between each in-breath and each out-breath, pause and find a moment of stillness. Practice gently slowing down your breath by increasing the length of your exhale. With each breath, let your heart become perfectly still. Let yourself surrender to a sense of stillness.

You're welcome to take as many heart breaths as you like to feel comfortable starting your practice. You can start with three heart breaths and then work your way up to ten heart breaths. If you need a place to focus your attention, keep practicing the heart breaths and pause between each inhale and exhale.

Practice: Heart Stillness

The heart is the center of awareness listening. While being present to all that's arising, practice listening inwardly to your heart, the seat of your divine consciousness. You can imagine a sacred flame burning brightly in the center. Watch the movement of the flame until it settles into complete stillness.

Heart stillness is the essence of the practice. When you feel stillness in your heart, you begin to experience stillness in your whole self. The fluctuations of prana become still. You find your mind more calm and your heart peaceful. Let this sense of stillness expand. See if you can anchor this energy of stillness and steadiness in your practice. Sit with stillness and allow it to permeate your being.

Let yourself feel supported by this sensation of complete universal centeredness. Take this experience of heart stillness with you throughout your day and notice how it nourishes you. With practice, this sense of steadiness will permeate every aspect of your daily life.

Practice: Heart Presence

You might think of presence in your mind, but presence is a whole experience of the soul, the heart, and the body. It extends beyond your mind; it includes your entire being.

In the space of heart stillness, take time to sense the radiance of your heart. You may envision this as a beautiful, sacred sphere of light extending out in all directions. Together with your heart breaths and stillness, become attuned to the presence of your heart.

Practice this by resting your attention in your heart. Notice how intending the presence of the heart allows you to feel more present. Observe how this sense of heart presence is different from the presence culti-vated by the mind.

Presence is a heightened state of attention in the moment. It's being here and nowhere else. Presence is healing. And healing helps you to become more present. The point of power is always in the NOW.

When you listen, you enter a state of receptivity. It shifts you from the thinking mind to an open state of being. In this space, let yourself observe. Give yourself full permission to listen without attachment or expec-tation. Let it be a time of receiving, and notice your experience — exactly as it is.

By resting in the heart, you move your focus from your mind to your divine center. In the space of the heart, you have greater access to expanded awareness, wisdom, and compassion.

Applying the Practice of Awareness

During your practice, let everything come to the surface of your awareness without resistance or attachment. Let your emotions, feelings, past memories, and thoughts rise without suppression. Let your true experience be as it is, and observe. When difficult thoughts arise, witness them. Breathe. Let them have space, but release yourself from having to do something about them. Just watch.

See your thoughts go by like clouds moving in the sky. Just as if you were watching a movie, sit back and observe your thoughts and feelings with a sense of curiosity and detachment. Observe yourself with compassion and understanding. The more you observe your own thoughts and feelings with loving kindness, the easier it becomes to see others through the lens of compassion.

In awareness meditation, welcome all that arises. Learn to embrace every moment, even the most intense resistance. In Flow, you allow all feelings and thoughts. Let yourself fully feel. Every experience is valuable, even the most challenging ones that are full of raw emotion. Embrace each experience as an old friend instead of trying to change it or push it away.

*Sura Flow is a
dynamic practice
that is deeply
healing.*

By experiencing your feelings and emotions exactly as they are, you connect to the truth of your experience. Good or bad, light or dark, right or wrong, experience what you feel without the label. Move beyond dual states of the mind and allow yourself to be with the full range of your existence without resistance.

Instead of avoiding, transcending, fixing, or changing, you find the courage to enter the center of your experience. This is where your liberation lies, in true presence. Be willing to enter the center of the pain, the darkness, the fear — the deep wound. Through practice, you learn to courageously face your thoughts and fears. It's in the dark places you'll discover your true self.

In Sura Flow, you learn how to have space for everything to exist as it is. You also learn to develop the skill of responding in the moment. When you accept your present moment, you're most empowered to shift it. By cultivating your awareness through meditation, you learn how to appreciate differences in experiences and perspective and to have space for everything to exist, as it is. Sura Flow is a dynamic practice that is deeply healing. If you need a place to land your attention during awareness listening, simply focus on the heart breaths, breathing in from the back of the heart and breathing out through the front of the heart. Be sure to pause between each in-breath and out-breath. Heart-centered listening is a time to allow, pay attention, and surrender to your true experience. It's a time of listening inward to what's present and true for you in the moment.

Visit *suraflow.org/practices* to receive a guided Sura Flow Heart meditation.

Receive Guidance and Wisdom From Within

When you're in flow, you're receptive to the energy of your spirit. When you become clear and still, you perceive more clearly. In meditation, you move beyond the limitations of the conditioned mind. Your thoughts begin to slow, and there's more space between each thought. In this space, you are open to receiving insight and guidance from your higher wisdom. This may come through as a direct insight or an "a-ha moment" or a simple knowing.

Pay attention to the subtle impressions from your practice. When the mind becomes placid and calm, like a still lake, you can receive the subtle vibrations from your practice. In this state, you're open to receiving energy and you become more subtle in your awareness. You may sense important messages and feelings that are vital to your own well-being.

Like a sacred vessel, you become an open space to receive the energy of calm and silence. In this space, it is easier to sense what's true for you. By residing in stillness, you not only experience deep peace, but you can hear the still inner voice. This kind of listening is also deeply nourishing and restorative.

By surrendering to stillness, you're open to receiving the nectar, the true bliss of meditation. You're tapping into your creative life force energy. It can feel like a deep spring that begins to bubble up from deep within your center. This spring feels joyful and fulfilling. It rejuvenates your entire being.

As you become steady through grounding and centering, you'll notice that it's easier to connect to inner stillness. The mind waves begin to slow and become quieter as you enter a state of bliss.

The Power of Inner Guidance

We were taught from a young age to listen to our parents. We were taught to listen to everyone, from society to teachers to the media — even God "out there." We have been taught to place our attention on the external authorities to know we're doing the right thing.

Awareness listening develops your skill to listen to guidance from *within*. Imagine having your own personal GPS system. Well, you do. It's already within you. You have everything you need to live your life skillfully. You have an immense spiritual resource that is constantly speaking with you and guiding you in the right direction.

From the place of quiet being in your center, you can receive direction and inspiration for your life path. The practice of listening allows you to access the still, quiet voice within. Your guidance is connected to *ALL THAT IS*. Your practice is a time to become attuned. It's about becoming spiritually connected and allowing yourself to be inwardly guided.

Awareness listening develops your skill to listen to guidance from within.

It is in this space of still, heart-centered listening that you connect to your true self. You may have stuffed some of this self down because you were afraid to fully be yourself. You might have been punished as a child just for being yourself. Someone may have questioned your perceptions and feelings. Or you may not have received validation or affirmation when you were growing up. Perhaps you were told you were "not enough" or "too much." You were scared to shine too bright for fear of being a target.

Sura Flow practice is not about becoming a perfect "spiritual" person who is "enlightened." Nor is it about being a "good boy or girl." It's not about being a saint or Mother Mary. It's about being yourself. It's the courage to live your true self. Who you are is unique.

There is no one like you. You are your own energy. As Joseph Campbell said, *"The privilege of a lifetime is being who you are."*

Sura Flow is a practice that nurtures you to live your whole, authentic self. You get to know this self over time through practice. Through meditation, you become aware of the parts of yourself that you may have denied or repressed simply because they are different. Perhaps there are parts of yourself you disowned because they were considered "weird" or "eccentric." As you develop in your practice, you'll find the unique characteristics of your soul begin to shine through. You discover the courage to be more daring, to take risks, and to be more particular. You feel safe to step out and be your own person.

The purpose of meditation is to become self-realized, to live your true, honest self. You will find that the more you meditate, the easier it is to listen to yourself and to know what's true for you. Through practice, you'll directly experience the knowledge and wisdom that already live within you. You'll develop the confidence to follow your own guidance. You'll know how to tap into the inherent creative intelligence that is constantly leading you on your unique, right path.

Awareness listening is a time of divine connection and communication. You may call it your divine self, God, or the universe. It's a time to tune in to the deeper rhythms and calling of your own heart. When you become disconnected from your spiritual self, you feel disconnected in your life. When you learn how to connect to your own spiritual center, you'll find everything you need is here and now.

The ability to connect to your creative intelligence is your birthright. If you have an intention or request, you're worthy of receiving an answer. It's not just for the elite few. Who you are is valuable. You are worthy of communicating with the divine, just like anyone else. Be transparent with the Universe. Let your heart speak freely. Trust that what comes to you is sacred. Know that you always have access to your own divine intelligence.

Be Open to Receiving

Listening is a skill you can learn to develop. You can become more subtle and sensitive in your ability to receive. With time, you may notice it becomes easier to tap into your creative, intuitive brain. Some people hear it like an audible message; others see visions. Some people feel it.

Be open to your creative insights, whatever they may be. They may at times seem odd or even "crazy." They can take you out of your comfort zone and for good reason — your inner guidance is here to help you grow spiritually.

Your creative insights may appear as an instant flash or as a subtle feeling. As you begin to trust your true experience during meditation, you'll also experience how liberating and empowering it is to take action on your intuition.

You could also refer to your inner guidance as inspiration, following your joy, or doing what feels right. It's an energy that's always available to you. It only takes a few moments to be quiet and listen, to receive divine direction in the moment. It feels natural, freeing. It can be spontaneous and even exciting. It's not something you need to think hard about. When you slow down and open up, your guidance comes to you.

> *Acting*
> *on your*
> *inner guidance*
> *empowers you to be*
> *free in expressing*
> *your true, whole*
> *self.*

By listening to your intuition and taking action on what feels true, you act on the power of your soul. It's the way your unique soul expression comes through you. Acting on your inner guidance empowers you to be free in expressing your true, whole self. It helps you embody your own spontaneous nature. This is the privilege of your practice: to realize who you already are. It gives you the courage to be yourself and to live your own true path.

Your guidance is a unique expression of who you are. When you act on what feels natural, true, and right to you, it's healing. It fortifies your spirit. You feel more embodied. You know it because you feel peaceful. Listening to your guidance strengthens your resilience. It empowers you to become more and more you.

Become a Clear Channel for Guidance to Flow Through

Your guidance has a resonance. It has a feeling of "rightness." When you listen to guidance, it feels like yielding to what's right. Your guidance can flow to you through any number of qualities, such as sight, sound, feeling, emotion, and energy. Some people describe it as a still, small voice.

People often wonder if what they are receiving is guidance or if it's just thoughts from their own mind. You'll notice, with time, that there's a difference between your regular thinking mind and your true inner guidance.

When you're receiving information from your spiritual creative brain, it often has a quality of love and expansiveness. When you receive it, you're likely to feel a sense of peace or relief. It leads you constantly toward love and wholeness. When you trust your guidance, it's an experience of surrender: a surrender to who you truly are.

Your creative intelligence is connected to the whole of consciousness (all that is). *It knows* information beyond your conscious, logical mind. Like the periscope of a submarine, your intuition can see far and wide in all directions above the water, whereas your conscious mind can only see a short distance directly in front of the submarine.

When you're receiving information from your regular thinking ego-mind, it has a different energetic quality. It may seem reasonable and logical, even good, but it lacks real energy. When you close your eyes and feel the essence of a mind-based piece of information, it can feel contracted or empty. These ideas are often grounded in fear and reason, including the need to protect ourselves and to look good to others. Oftentimes, ego-mind ideas are based on logic or past experience.

When you tune in to your personal guidance, you know it is right because the energy flows. When it comes through, it feels fluid, natural. It does not feel heavy or torqued. When you receive it and *act* on it, you energetically feel lighter and more aligned.

Intuition Can See Far and Wide

Guidance can seem "unreasonable" to the logical, conscious mind, but with it comes a feeling of originality. It's fresh. Your intuition often takes you to new places so that you can grow. It can encourage you to take risks you'd never consider, but deep down, you know when you're being called. Your power is in your response. You alone have the capacity to act on your inner callings. No one else can hear them for you. Your guidance flows from within and helps you evolve.

"In prayer, it is better to have a heart without words than words without a heart."
— *Mahatma Gandhi*

Practice: Heart Guidance

You can tune in to your divine guidance through your heart center. Take a moment and close your eyes. Think of a problem or decision you need to make. Take three heart breaths. Become quiet and still in your heart, then envision one of the choices you're pondering. What do you feel in your heart? Do you notice a feeling of expansion or contraction? Does it feel tense or empty? Is it harder or easier to breathe?

Oftentimes, if the answer to the bigger question you're asking is a "yes," you feel a strengthening and expansion in your heart. It feels calm, connected, real. When it's a "no," you feel an empty, "off" feeling. A "no" can also be reflected by tension or even feeling out of your body. You can practice this by taking three heart breaths and then saying, "yes," to feel a "yes" response from your heart center. Pause and notice what you feel. Do the same for a "no," and notice what a "no" response feels like.

Your focused imagination together with heart feeling will guide you in the right direction. Your body is a powerful instrument attuned to your personal truth. If you listen, you will notice that your energy is always communicating to you. You have an incredible resource within you where you can access your own divine information.

Truth is a vibration. Your electromagnetic field will tell you what is right for you. Your electricity or chi will feel stronger and more connected when you're connected to your truth.

Try this exercise when you want to know the truth of your deeper wisdom: place one hand on your heart and say, "my heart says..." Notice what flows out of your heart and into your words. You may be surprised at what your heart really knows.

What does your heart clearly want?

The more your trust your intuition and follow it, the stronger this "muscle" becomes. It's a vital life skill that keeps you protected and leads you in the right direction. It can be helpful to name this part of your consciousness that represents your divine guidance. Sonia Choquette, a wonderful teacher and guide, calls her intuition "bright light." By naming anything, including the quality of your guidance, you develop a stronger relationship with it.

When you name your resources, you strengthen them. You clarify the energy that becomes available to you. You develop a stronger awareness and connection with it. Practice listening to your intuition daily. Name it, talk with it, write to it daily. It's an important practice that nourishes your inner self. It bolsters your spirit and keeps you fresh. It opens up your channel and keeps you flowing with all of life.

When you follow your own true self, you become the true leader of your life. You are the creator of your life. One of your greatest powers is the power of your choice. As a divine creator, you get to choose what's important, what to take action on, and how to focus your time and energy. You can be anything. You can do anything. Through regular Flow practice, you can learn how to cast aside fears and judgments so you can live freely.

The more you practice Sura Flow, the more confidence and courage you will nurture in yourself. When you take time to raise your self-awareness, question the thoughts you've always had, and examine beliefs like "not being good enough," you become empowered to shift. Meditation creates a disruption in your normal mode of thinking. It teaches you to listen to what's emerging within. When you trust your own perceptions, your own feelings, and your own sense of inner direction, life takes on a truly magic quality.

Instead of resisting life, you'll discover that accepting life as it is — and accepting yourself as you are — is deeply empowering. By facing life as it is, you'll learn how to flow and harmonize with life instead of feeling overwhelmed by it. Releasing judgment and resistance gives you energy. Acceptance paradoxically empowers you to create positive change. Your meditation will connect you deeply to your present-moment reality, giving you inspiration and unlimited energy potential.

You are the
creator
of your life.

Heal Your Energy

During meditation, you cultivate a quality of energy. It has been shown that through meditative practice, you develop coherence. When you are in a state of coherence, you harmonize. Your mind, body, and emotions become balanced. You get in touch with your natural biorhythms and give yourself permission to follow them. This includes the coherence that emanates from your heart. It raises your vibration and creates harmonic balance throughout your body.

Think of this state of coherence as a smooth, bonded energy flow cultivated from being in stillness. Meditation allows you to bond to the energy of spiritual chi, your own life force energy. The more you meditate, the more you access your own subtle "light" body. Through practice, you can live and embody your spiritual energy.

When you experience trauma or intense stress, you can experience soul loss and with that a loss of spiritual energy. When this happens, parts of your soul become disconnected or fragmented. During an intense trauma, you may become disassociated (split apart) from your body in order to cope. It's a natural survival mechanism that keeps you from feeling the full brunt of trauma, but in the process, you lose parts of yourself.

You may have experienced certain major events and losses in life and realized that you weren't quite the same after. You might have lost that spark or feeling of joy. It's common to lose a sense of yourself after a major stressful life event like death or a break-up. You may have felt a loss of vitality and happiness. During stressful or traumatic events, it can take a while to return to yourself. You may feel listless, groundless, and dispirited. These experiences are a sign of soul loss.

The Sura Flow practice is a natural healing approach that takes into consideration the healing of the soul. More than watching your thoughts, you can reclaim your spiritual power and energy so you feel more centered, whole, and balanced energetically. You will notice that you feel more "together" and focused after practicing some of the healing tools. You will feel more viscerally the center of your being. The energy practices offered through relaxation and heart listening allow you to heal at a soul level across all time, space, and dimensions.

CHAPTER 19

INTENTION

*"Each decision we make, each action we take,
is born out of an intention."*
— **Sharon Salzberg**

While you meditate, you can gather spiritual force and consciously invite it into your body. Think of it as creating a compact capsule of your own chi. You become focused and laser-like. During Flow practice, you can build your energy and vitality, which helps you to cultivate beauty, longevity, and presence.

When you gather your life force energy, you can apply this renewed, focused energy toward a higher purpose. When you're in a state of non-resistance and complete peace, it's the perfect time to focus on a positive intention. Your intention will set more deeply in your consciousness when you're in a state of oneness.

The end of your Sura Flow practice is an ideal time to say a prayer, a blessing, or set an intention. During this time, you can also offer up healing. When you are present and centered, you can effortlessly flow healing energy. The end of a meditation is a potent time for manifestation. In a deeper, more connected consciousness state, your healing intention becomes magnified. You may discover that in this state, you are so connected that you can instantly manifest your deeper desires.

> *The end of a meditation is a potent time for manifestation.*

Find Your Intention

Flow meditation provides a clear vision of finding your deepest desires. Ask yourself, "What do I really want?" Tune in to your heart and meditate on your true inner desire.

The key is to listen and be completely open. Be aware of the mind's tendency to limit your desire. Oftentimes, people are ashamed of admitting what they really want. It's "too big," they think. "What will others think?" allows the fear of judgment to creep in. Your desires are yours alone. Your desires are divine.

Questions to discover your true desires:

- What do I truly want to experience in this lifetime?
- If I had a month to live, what would I do?
- What is most important to me?
- What does my soul want?

Take time to meditate on your life intention. Sit and journal these questions. Practice heart awareness and wait for the right information to flow to you. When you discover your life intention, tune in to the state of being that you most want to experience. With that in mind, be sure to focus on the positive outcome you want to create. For example, instead of saying, "I don't want to be stressed," you would intend, "I am peace."

Your intention is a heartfelt prayer. It emanates from the level of your soul. It's meaningful because it says something about how you want to live your life. Your intention is an internal guide for living your best life and achieving your potential. By having a proactive intention, your chances of experiencing it increase dramatically. It also helps to write down your intention and keep it near you at all times where you can see it.

Guidelines to manifest your intention:

1. You really want it.
2. You feel spiritually connected to it.
3. It is clear and focused.

The key to creating a strong intention is to create a clear, simple statement in the *present tense*. This sends a message to your subconscious brain during your meditation that it has been created in the now. A few examples are, "I'm a clear channel for peace," or "I'm a creative artist." Positive intentions uplift your energy and state of being. They make you feel more like *you*.

Sample Qualities of Strong Intentions

Healthy	*Fulfilled*	*Forgiving*
Joy	*Peaceful*	*Happy*
Positive	*Equality*	*Light*
Balanced	*Stable*	*Secure*
Open	*Loving*	*Confident*
Creative	*Purposeful*	*Energetic*
Freedom	*Strong*	*Loving*

Intentions to offer at the end of your Sura Flow meditation:

I am peace.

I am calm.

I am balanced.

I am bliss.

I am love.

I am infinite.

I am eternal.

I am divine.

I am one with the divine.

Healing blessings for humanity.

May we all be free.

May we all be peaceful.

Practice: Intention Setting

When focusing on your intentional thoughts, let yourself rest easy in your center. You can even envision that universal energy is centering you, so *you* don't have to do anything. It happens by itself through your awareness. You simply allow yourself to be centered, to be grounded in your intention. In your heart center, let yourself gently focus on your intention. As you do, you may start to notice some energy shifts or even the feeling of peace.

Clearly feel and state your intention in your heart center. Pay attention to what you experience when you set your intention. Notice the sensations and emotions, and your mental state. What is the experience like? What subtle energy shifts do you notice?

Let yourself fully feel the energy of your desired creation. Allow there to be a sense of ease and spaciousness. You may sense a continuing energy shift. You may even notice that once your intention has been "set" or "created," you experience a feeling of completion. You can also set your intention by letting yourself imagine that your intention has already happened. Immerse yourself in the full sensation, experience, emotions, and feelings of your completed intention.

> *Clearly feel and state your intention in your heart center.*

Our intentions are healing. Like the center of a mandala that extends outward into a beautiful circular geometric pattern, you set the seed of your intention through stillness. Your intentions create an energetic ripple effect that extends out into the energy field.

Mandala

You can sense when the energy has finished for your intention setting. There's often a deep sense of peace and completion. It's like sensing when a cake has finished baking in the oven. The energy begins to run out. The energy behind your intention becomes even as it integrates with the field. That's when you can intuitively feel your intention has "set." The final step is to surrender your intention completely, knowing that the Universe has received your order. Accept your intention as if it has already happened. You can do this with a simple gesture of gratitude, such as a bow. At the end, you can affirm, "thy (divine) will be done. Namaste."

Just as you plant a seed in the ground, in order for it to grow, you leave the intention alone. If you keep doubting or questioning your creative intentions, it's like digging up the seed over and over again. It doesn't allow your desire to take root and grow. You've got to leave the seed alone so it can blossom on its own. This takes faith and patience.

*The magic is in
the action.*

Once you've set your intention, trust that the Universe will take care of it in divine time. In creating through your Flow practice, remember to practice detachment. By releasing your personal energy around your creation, you give it space to breathe and create new life. Trust that this energy has been set within you and in the field.

Another key is to take action steps toward realizing your intention. If you want to be a successful artist, then commit to creating art. The art won't be made by itself; it's up to you to take new actions toward your creative aspirations. The magic is in the action.

Author James Redfield said, *"Where attention goes Energy flows; Where intention goes Energy flows!"*

Be mindful of both your attention and your energy after you've set an intention. Are you acting, speaking, and being in alignment with what you say you want to create? Are you truly embodying your life intention?

If you've affirmed you want to be a successful artist, do you keep neglecting your own work? Or are you willing to commit to yourself as an artist? Notice if there are any incongruences in your speech, actions, and intentions. The key to unleashing your creative power is to raise your awareness and align all parts of yourself to your creative intention.

*Intentions
are healing.*

Lastly, let go and be present in your everyday life. Notice what happens without judgment. Be open to receiving guidance at any time during your day. When you get some free space, ask Spirit, "What would be joyful? What should I do now?" Listen to what flows to you and be open. Stay in a high vibrational state by being mindful of your energy and being balanced throughout your day. This moment-to-moment awareness attunes you to your higher self and your inner guidance.

Setting your intention is like sending out a radio signal. Listening is like being the radio receiver. You dial into a specific station when you focus on your intention. You become "tuned" in to that creative possibility, and then you begin to receive the energy frequencies needed to realize your intention. Consider it a two-way communication. You cast your intention, and then you listen to your intuitive guidance. The key to manifesting your intention is to be receptive to what comes to you — and to act on it. It takes trust and courage.

Intentions are healing. They change you on a cellular level. Every intention creates a subtle inner change within you. They change your energy. They shift your consciousness. This is because your energetic field responds to your intentions and becomes attuned to your internal focus. What you focus on matters. Maintaining an awareness of your thoughts, living a healthy lifestyle, and keeping good company are instrumental to living a high-vibrational life. You'll find that by staying in positive flow and by living in harmony with life your intentions manifest by themselves. Don't be surprised if you experience heightened synchronicity and unexpected miracles.

Practice: Meditation Circles

The power of intention expands when you meditate with others. Ideally, you will find time to consistently meditate with a teacher and group that resonate with you. It will not only help you develop your own practice, but it's a joyful way to spend time with your community. Choose to meditate once a week or once a month in a group.

Committing to your own practice, while being in community, is a powerful way to integrate your Sura Flow practice.

Closing Your Sura Flow Meditation Practice

When you complete your practice, I highly recommend intentionally closing it. This can be as simple as stating inwardly to yourself, "my practice is complete." I recommend taking a moment to become aware of its sacred offering and formally close your practice with a bow, a short prayer, or even a sacred sound. By concluding and acknowledging your meditation, you affirm that you completed your practice.

It may happen that when you meditate, you get up afterwards, feel more expansive, and are still engaged in your meditation practice. Your practice may be so casual that there is no clear point between your sitting session and the rest of your day. You can even feel floaty, still in an open, "meditative state." Or you may experience lingering thoughts about your sitting practice, such as, "Did I meditate well enough?"

It helps cultivate confidence in having completed a wonderful action of your day, such as making your bed. You feel a sense of accomplishment. It not only helps create a container for your practice but also gives you a sense of completion.

To close your practice, you can make an internal or an external gesture. You can do this by internally saying, "thank you" or "namaste" to acknowledge the gift of the practice. You can also make a physical gesture, such as bowing, an act of reverence and surrender. You can seal your aura and ground yourself to the Earth to protect this newfound vibration you received from your practice.

By closing your practice, you complete that action of meditation and transition to the next part of your day, with full presence.

CHAPTER 20

SUPPLEMENTARY PRACTICE
— DIVINE NOTES

Divine notes is a supplementary practice I developed when I first started reading Julia Cameron's *The Artist's Way*. In this book, she introduces the practice of "morning pages," which is writing three pages in a stream of consciousness first thing in the morning. When you write, you jot down anything that comes to mind. Even if nothing comes, you can write, "I don't know what to write. This is silly." You might write about your dreams or about the day's events.

When I first started morning pages, writing three stream-of-consciousness pages seemed like a frivolous exercise, but I kept with it. With time, I saw that there was magic to this practice.

This seemingly simple writing practice was profoundly life-changing. I found it to be very healing, revealing the deepest, darkest parts of my own psyche. Writing down my thoughts each day became a meditation in motion. I could see more clearly what was in my own mind and what was burdening my heart. I wrote more boldly about my own pain and what I wanted to resolve. Eventually,

I garnered the courage to write about my own deepest desires and what I wanted to create for myself in my life.

It was a safe place to fully express myself. When I felt hard emotions or experiences come up, I started writing about them in my morning pages. After some time writing my morning pages, I started to receive revelatory insights into my pleas for help. I began writing in a flow state. It was like a divine force moving through my pen, guiding me to the answers I most needed to hear. I felt empowered. It allowed me to tap into a benevolent, wise guide.

Eventually, these pages became a way for me to communicate with my divine self. Sometimes, I would write a question I was pondering, a topic I really wanted to understand. I'd write the question and then wait for a bit. I'd become receptive by letting go. Then I'd start writing anything that came through. Sometimes, I didn't even know what I was going to write. There's always a moment of uncertainty that's there.

This way of writing can be a vulnerable process. There are moments of groundlessness. Even so, with this process I was always astonished at the wisdom and insight that I would eventually write. Whatever I needed would always come through my writing.

It took me years to realize that I could always go to the page and find a comforting answer that made me feel better. To access this writing flow state, all I needed to do was relax and trust. There was, of course, often a moment of self-doubt. But if I stayed with it and allowed the process, I would always receive some response that uplifted me and helped me to understand, to be more open and compassionate. When I wrote in this way, wisdom flowed from my hand and onto the page.

Every one of us can be an open channel for divine wisdom. Divine notes is a method of flow. It's just in the form of writing; a way of channeling the truth that already exists within you.

Divine notes are similar to morning pages. The way you practice divine notes consists of writing what's in your heart, then waiting and responding from a place of allowing. At first, it can feel like an uncomfortable process. It's meant to be. You're opening up to an aspect of your consciousness and tapping in. Through divine notes, you're unlocking a channel inside of you, a way of effortlessly expressing your own divine wisdom. You are tapping into your inner-knowing.

Divine notes is a method of flow.

In divine notes, you are channeling your own wisdom. You may have read the wonderful *Conversations with God* books by Neale Donald Walsch. We all have this ability to speak to God, the Universe, our higher wisdom. It starts with intention. It develops with practice and commitment.

Meditation opens the way to accessing deeper parts of your innate wisdom. Divine notes put your practice into action. It's a tool to connect you to your own Source. We all have the divine spark within us. We all have access to our own divine knowledge. Divine notes is a revelatory process. Here are guidelines to encourage you through this daily practice.

Writing Your Divine Notes:

- Commit to writing at least two pages a day or for ten minutes straight. Do this first thing in the morning before meditation. Write in journals that have plenty of space to write freely. I love to write in simple composition books because they have plenty of space and are inexpensive!
- Imagine that you're writing to someone who is unconditionally present and supportive. This could be God, a best friend, or a spirit guide.
- Write about your deepest thoughts and concerns. Write about what's most on your heart or something you truly want to explore and understand.
- Start with a statement or a question about what you want guidance on.
- Wait and notice what flows to you intuitively. What do you feel like writing? Trust yourself and let yourself write freely without judgment, editing, or analysis.
- Close your practice by writing an intention for your day.

CHAPTER 21

SURA FLOW IN EVERYDAY LIFE
HOW TO BEGIN A PRACTICE

Divine Notes Practice

Each morning, write two pages minimum or for ten minutes straight upon waking up. Continue writing until you feel complete.

Sura Flow Practice

After divine notes, practice Sura Flow meditation for at least ten minutes. Begin with relaxation, then practice listening, and close with your heartfelt intention. You can apply hands-on healing for the entirety of your practice. Within a month, work toward twenty minutes of meditation in your day. The ideal amount of time for meditation is thirty minutes for more experienced practitioners.

I highly recommend completing your divine notes and Flow meditation practices first thing in the morning when you are clear, before you begin the engagements of your day. Starting from a place of center and balance sets the tone for the whole day.

End Your Day with Energy Balancing

Release extra energy by grounding and letting go of all the activity of your day. Fill your life force energy back up with universal energy. You can practice hands-on healing to rebalance the energy flowing through your body. Ten minutes is a good amount of time to dedicate to this practice. Consider increasing this amount to twenty to thirty minutes in the evening. You can always adjust for what works best for your energy and schedule.

CHAPTER 22

SYNCHRONICITY, GUIDANCE,
AND UNEXPECTED MIRACLES

*"I am open to the guidance of synchronicity,
and do not let expectations hinder my path"*
— **Dalai Lama**

The day after Christmas in 2004, my life took an unexpected turn. I was getting ready to go on a big trip to Koh Phi Phi Island in Thailand to learn more about meditation and Buddhism. That day the massive tsunami hit Asia. The resort I had been scheduled to stay on, Charlie Beach Resort, was hit hard — there were no survivors.

The news devastated me. Hundreds of thousands of people had been killed. I felt incredibly guilty for having survived this tragic event. A huge range of emotions moved through me, and I cried many tears of sadness and grief.

That brush with death was disturbing, but it was also a blessing in disguise.

For the first time, I thought about what I really wanted to do with my life. I asked myself, "What would I do with a second chance in life?" I started wondering if I had a purpose.

Shortly after, I canceled my trip to Asia and booked a new one to Costa Rica. It was a place I felt guided to go. It was there, near San Jose at a yoga retreat called Pura Vida, that I found myself having an unexpected emotional breakdown during yoga class.

While doing a triangle pose, I began sobbing. It was as if a dam broke inside my body. I crumpled onto my mat and cried for the rest of the class. When class was over, everyone left. The teacher came back into the room with a box of tissues. She didn't say a word; she set them down and quietly left. In that moment, everything I held onto in my life started to melt away. The retreat at Pura Vida was deeply healing. I knew my life was about to change, but I had no idea what I was going to do.

Since I really enjoyed the yoga retreat there, I asked one of the instructors if she could recommend a yoga teacher training. She was a petite, blonde-haired woman. She simply said, "Yes, Nosara." Huh? My energy dropped. I was disappointed because I had never heard of it before. She seemed to sense my confusion, so she wrote it down on a piece of paper for me. I looked at the name again and folded the paper up to take with me to my tent. Afterward, I threw it in my bag and forgot about it.

That week, after I arrived back home in New York City, I spontaneously decided to see one of my favorite Buddhist monks, Geshe Michael Roach. He was speaking at a church in Midtown, so I dropped my travel bags from Costa Rica and took the subway from Brooklyn to see him give a talk. Afterward, I waited in the long line of people who wanted to greet Geshe Michael personally.

As I waited, I noticed a woman standing behind me who looked like an angel. She was tall with long, large curls. She was very peaceful and seemed to have an ethereal glow about her. I became curious and finally turned around to start up a conversation. I asked her the typical New York question, "What do you do?" She said, "I teach yoga to cancer patients." Her response sent a chill down my spine. It seemed like a very honorable vocation. I responded, "Where did you learn how to do that?" She looked at me and said, "Nosara."

Hadn't I heard that name before? It sounded really familiar. I ran home that evening from the subway station. When I got home, I tore through the bags that were still packed. From inside one of the pockets, I pulled out the piece of paper from the yoga teacher at Pura Vida. It said, "Nosara."

I ran to my computer and got on the internet to Google "Nosara." I clicked on "Founders" and read about Don and Amba Stapleton. A strange familiarity came over me. The hair on the back of my neck started to stand. I tore through the stack of books piled high behind me. I quickly uncovered *Self-Awakening Yoga* by Don Stapleton. It was a book I cherished. It was the first and only book I had ever read on yoga. Don, the author, is the founder of Nosara Yoga in Costa Rica.

I was shocked by this strange occurrence of seemingly unrelated events that all pointed to one yoga destination: Nosara, a small surf town on the Pacific coast of Costa Rica.

I knew I had to go there. The more I learned about Nosara, the more I wanted to do my yoga training there. But it seemed completely unrealistic, like an airy fairy dream. I had massive responsibility at work. It just so happened that my company had simultaneously promoted me to partner, and I was set to open a new office for them in San Francisco. Now I had to go and undo all that. When I walked into one of the partners' office to tell him I needed to go do yoga training, he exclaimed, "Why do you have to go all the way to Costa Rica?? Are you crazy??"

People at the office started calling me crazy. They wondered if I was having a mid-life, existential crisis. Everyone called me crazy because of the huge amounts of money I was walking away from. But the feeling of needing to leave New York haunted me. I started losing sleep. I felt like something bad would happen if I stayed in my current job on Wall Street. Then one day I called my mom and told her that I wanted to go to Nosara. She said, "Follow your heart and don't look back."

That was the extra bit of encouragement I needed to take a leap of faith. I decided to quit my job, sell all my things, and rent out my condo. From the moment I decided to leave New York, everything flowed effortlessly. I sold every piece of furniture to the first interested buyer, rented my place to the first couple who saw it, and gave over my multi-million-dollar book of business to a brand-new vice president of sales. The biggest miracle was finding a parking space for the size of a moving van — right in front of my building's doorway.

Trusting and following synchronicity has taken me on an adventure of a lifetime. It has led me to experiences beyond what I could have imagined for myself. There's an intelligence that expresses itself through synchronicity, especially when you learn how to pay attention and follow it.

When I worked in the corporate world, I had a more linear path laid out in front of me. It was secure, it was solid, but it wasn't mine. The trajectory of that path made me feel hollow. It wasn't until I trusted the message of synchronicity that I found the courage to live my own life.

Guidance and Synchronicity Are Interconnected

Over time, I've discovered there's an inexplicable connection between inner guidance and synchronicity.

The more you follow your intuition, the more likely you are to experience synchronicity. Listening to your intuition is like having a direct line to the magic flow of life. The feeling of guidance is like a quiet inner joy that flows from within. When you're truly open and present, unattached to any particular outcome, you're available to enter the natural flow of life.

When you experience a meaningful coincidence, it uplifts you. It affirms you're on the right path. Synchronicities are miracles. For a moment, you've transcended, connected to something bigger than yourself. You are in flow with all of life.

Synchronicity has been called a "God wink." Oftentimes, you feel a sense of validation when you experience it. You just know you're on the right path. The concept was first introduced by Swiss psychologist Carl Jung, who coined the term synchronicity to describe a "meaningful coincidence." Jung technically defined synchronicity as "temporally coincident occurrences of acausal events," which boils down to a pattern of connection that cannot be explained through cause. In other words, a random event may not be random but rather a reflection of a higher order.

Synchronicities are miracles.

There's an intelligence that flows through this order. It exists for a reason. Synchronicity helps transform your consciousness from an ego-centric point of view to a more enlightened, balanced perspective. When you experience this deep, unusual interconnectedness through meaningful coincidence, you understand that there is a larger picture at play. There is divine order.

Synchronicity is an opportunity to grow spiritually. All synchronistic experiences are unique, but there are some that deeply touch you. Once I read about a man in New York who had lost touch with his daughter, only to discover thirteen years later that the whole time they had lived a mile and a half from each other. These kinds of deeper coincidences move you emotionally. When you feel the profound emotional effect of synchronicity, take time to meditate on your experience. What is it telling you? How is it guiding you?

Synchronistic events can propel you toward your own true life path and purpose, guiding you readily toward your destiny. You'll begin to notice patterns in your experiences that reveal to you your next steps. This is especially true during major life changes when you're more receptive to "signs" from the Universe. This, as well as in times of deep healing, is when synchronicity can be most potent. When you allow miraculous events to guide you, it activates your potential. It makes you pay attention. By allowing synchronicity to unfold in your life, you feel connected to a higher power. You are connected to the oneness of life.

When you listen to hidden messages in your synchronistic experiences, you enter the mystery of life. You become part of a mysterious creation constantly leading you into the unknown toward bigger, greater aspects of yourself. These experiences lead you on an evolutionary, unexpected pathway. They lead you to miracles beyond your imagination.

When you examine the patterns through your meaningful coincidences, and integrate them into your own life path, you raise your consciousness. Many of these patterns may be archetypal and energetic in nature. For example, if you find yourself dealing with the archetype of "bully," and you are the constant "victim," then these patterned experiences are asking you to transform to reclaim your power. This helps you heal and expand your own consciousness.

Synchronistic experiences can be positive or negative. Repeated experiences and patterns can provide context for your own healing and growth. They keep showing up for a reason. It's up to you to notice them and decide how you want to respond to these experiences. Oftentimes, they offer an opportunity to discover where you need to cultivate balance within yourself in order to evolve.

When your personal life experiences begin to accelerate through synchronicity, you feel as though you're surfing the waves of life. You can feel the universal wind behind your back. Your intentions manifest effortlessly. You experience divine miracles. You are living in your flow. You are living your soul power.

When you follow your divine guidance, you develop confidence and a deep inner peace and knowing. The stress falls away. It is a way of life that extends beyond the logical mind and into the way of the heart. When you're connected to your true inner flow, you begin to notice more synchronicity unfold in your life. You connect to "all that is" in your creative actions. You are free to sit back, relax, and let magic happen.

Synchronicity demonstrates the oneness of life. It shows you that miracles exist and that they are connected to listening to your inner-guidance. It offers you healing, growth, and expanded awareness. It shows you how truly united we all are. You can learn from your synchronistic experiences by paying attention to them and writing about them in your divine notes. This helps you integrate the wisdom gleaned from your experience, notice more patterns such as through your dreams, and track your personal progress. Pay attention to your synchronicities.

Reflection questions for synchronistic experiences:

- When were the times in your life you experienced synchronicity?
- What have your experiences of synchronicity shown you?
- What is synchronicity telling you about your life path?

"According to Vedanta, there are only two symptoms of enlightenment, just two indications that a transformation is taking place within you toward a higher consciousness. The first symptom is that you stop worrying. Things don't bother you anymore. You become light hearted and full of joy. The second symptom is that you encounter more and more meaningful coincidences in your life, more and more synchronicities. And this accelerates to the point where you actually experience the miraculous."

— **Deepak Chopra**

CHAPTER 23

MEDITATION COACHING

One day, I was sitting on a beach on Koh Samui, Thailand. I was drinking a coconut when I heard this gentle message, "Sura... It's time to go back and teach what you've learned." This message was not only a surprise, but it was the last thing I wanted to hear. I enjoyed my free-spirited life in Asia. I woke up, practiced yoga, went to the beach, and connected with friends. There were no responsibilities. I had zero plans to return to the United States. Aside from that, I responded to that message with "Teach what?" I couldn't imagine teaching anything that I had learned.

When I finally returned from studying in Asia, the time came when I had to face reality and get a job. I considered going back to a corporate job in the United States. After all, I needed to make money. It was the responsible thing to do. But every time I tried to pick up the phone to call a potential employer, I broke down in tears. Something deep inside me resisted going back to work in New York, but I had no idea what I was going to do to make a living.

During that time, I had started executive coaching school at Georgetown University in Washington, D.C. I had applied there at the suggestion of my previous finance clients who said I should be a life coach. It was because I loved helping people. Coaching seemed like a good skill to have.

While I was staying on the East Coast, one of my old clients from Wall Street called me. Steve was a hedge fund CEO based in New York City. He said, "I'm stressed out. Can you come over and show me what you learned in Asia? You look peaceful. I really need some of that."

"Some of… what?" I asked.

He said, "Whatever you do to be peaceful, I need to learn that."

I was surprised by his request and wasn't sure how to respond. How was I going to show a hedge fund CEO how to practice yoga and meditate? What would we do?

On a weekday afternoon, I met Steve at his Midtown office. I checked in through security and took the elevator up to his floor. Going in, I still didn't have a clear idea of how I'd help him. When I arrived, I invited him to sit down with me on his carpeted office floor. That's how we started: we both sat on the floor, moving and stretching. I helped him stretch by supporting and pushing his back.

We moved through several simple yoga sequences. He seemed more relaxed after each posture. After we finished yoga, I gave him energy healing. Then we sat on his office floor in silent meditation for ten minutes.

When we were finished, Steve quietly got up, stretched his arms out and said, "Ahh, I feel so good." He left the office. I was sitting there wondering what he had experienced and if he thought it was too weird for him.

It was the first time I had practiced yoga, coaching, meditation, and healing at once. It wound up being an experimental experience since I didn't know what I was really doing. Yet, I discovered that somehow it all flowed together beautifully.

Steve came back with a check in his hand. He reached over and handed it to me. I asked him, "What's this?"

He said, with tears in his eyes, "*This* is your work in the world."

I was stunned. I hadn't expected him to pay me. But he insisted, saying, "You're going to be like Tony Robbins." At that time, I didn't know who Tony Robbins was, but I didn't say anything.

Steve officially became my first client. He was very open. He allowed me to fully experiment and refine my offerings as an executive coach. It was always a flow, an art. I discovered how much I loved teaching meditation and coaching with clients. In a short amount of time, Steve's practice took root and he began practicing consistently.

Over the course of several years, Steve became a serious meditation practitioner. I saw the light in his eyes and a gentle peace radiating from his heart. He was very drawn to the practice. Eventually he quit his work as a hedge fund manager. Steve retired and became a hospice chaplain. Eventually he became a philanthropist for mindfulness in healthcare.

Working with Steve laid the foundation for working with other executive clients. It gave me the confidence and inspiration to start new work in the path of serving others.

The Power of Groups

When I moved to Los Angeles, Steve referred me to a few clients, and I began to teach yoga and meditation. It wasn't long after that I began auditioning at studios, and one in particular was an executive club in Century City. After I taught the manager a class, she offered me a teaching position on the spot. When I arrived on a Sunday to teach my first class, I saw my name posted on the schedule; it said, "Restorative yoga and meditation - Sura."

My heart sank. It sent me into a mini-panic. Firstly, I did not know how to teach restorative yoga. And secondly, I had no idea how to teach meditation. So I walked into class that day making up poses as I went, feeling insecure and unsure about what I was doing. Then I did what I could to guide a calming meditation. I made it all up as I went and felt like a fraud.

Afterward, I spoke to the director about teaching such a class I had no real experience in, she frankly said, "Well, that's the vibe I got from you." I sighed and realized I'd have to figure something out. Since there were very limited online resources I could find back then, I had to teach myself how to teach meditation.

Before moving to Los Angeles, I had never taught meditation in a group setting. So I decided to teach what I had learned as a beginner: counting breaths from 10 to 1. It was surprisingly effective. I discovered how joyful it was to lead meditation for a group. I felt a sense of calm and joy beyond words. It was different from my own individual practice. It allowed me to experience peace on a whole new level.

It wasn't until I started teaching meditation coaching that I truly understood the power of groups and meditating in a group. After teaching classes for several years, I was asked to "teach that combo you do: meditation, coaching, and healing." People began asking to be trained to do what I did, but there really wasn't a name for it, so I started calling it "Integrated Life Coach Training," and several years later, it evolved into "Certified LIBERATE Meditation Coaching."

Every step along my path, I was asked to up-level and teach. In the beginning I told people, "I'm not a yoga teacher" and "I'm not a meditation teacher." Perhaps I did this because I didn't want to disappoint people. If I wasn't an expert, they would not expect too much from me, but eventually I noticed that no one really seemed to care about that. In the beginning I was asked to teach yoga, then meditation, then healing, then professional certified meditation training courses. This happened no matter where in the world I was. As soon as I mentioned meditation, people wanted to learn.

When people started requesting meditation life coach trainings, I wasn't sure what to do. I was traveling and mostly in retreat. But I felt guided to say YES. So I said, "Okay, let's do a six-month training together." I used what I had with me, my laptop. The whole training was taught through a free teleconferencing line and email. I had no idea how it would turn out or if it would actually work. But much to everyone's surprise, including my own, the energy of meditation was transmitted through the air waves. Every time we sat together, we felt more peaceful, more connected, more ourselves.

This is how our meditation trainings began. It was very simple and accessible. There was no commute, no hassle, no rent or spaces to deal with. Eventually I had a vision for sharing meditation trainings via video conference so I could connect with people more readily. Teaching online was a way to stay connected and continue to share without having to be tied to a physical location. Being online also allowed me to stay in my own retreat at Salt Spring Island, BC.

When I started teaching online meditation in 2015, people often asked, "How do you do that?" I received a lot of doubt and questions about it being real. Many people doubted that it was a viable way to teach meditation, having been comfortable with the traditional means of instruction and practice.

Indeed, you can receive the transmission of healing and meditation from anywhere. Energy is boundless. It is unlimited, transcending both space and time. When people experience training online, it is highly effective, though some still prefer to learn meditation in person. As someone who has taught both ways and continues to see the benefits of in-person and online,

I still love the opportunity of teaching online due to its efficiency and global reach.

By the time the Covid-19 pandemic hit in 2020, online was our sole way of teaching and it became a clear avenue for sharing during a time of social distancing. One of our greatest joys is sharing Sura Flow meditation in groups. It brings a profound sense of collective calm especially when an entire group is focused on a positive intention. The energy expands.

Energy is boundless.

Groups of geese flying together cover longer distances than they could alone. Meditating together in a group creates a similar effect; you go deeper and higher than you would on your own. I highly suggest you practice on your own, in addition to being with a like-minded group.

The times we have led groups and participated in group meditations, we've all experienced deep levels of bliss and transcendence together. A group experience allows you to tap into a deep reservoir of peace, and like birds of a feather who fly together, you carry one another through the practice. The deeper healing opportunity is profound.

Leading a group meditation practice is incredibly joyful. You don't have to be an expert in meditation to start a meditation circle. As you can see, my path developed from little to no experience. All you need is willingness to share the practice. Most of the experience can be silent.

You'll find that by consistently being part of a community, you receive a deeper level of understanding your practice. In facilitating meditation, you receive a boost to your own personal energy system. It adds to your spiritual resource, inspires your own practice, and supports your health. It also gives you a strength beyond words, a sacred strength, one that helps you develop clarity, focus, and resilience.

*In a group,
you amplify the
energy field.*

I have found that by meditating in groups, your own ability to heal and manifest accelerates. This is because you're coming together to enter a flow state. A group that sits together in coherence and focuses on a single, positive intention can realize that intention more readily than a person could do on his/her own. In a group, you amplify the energy field. You'll discover that the act of sitting in a group together consistently will allow things in your own life to manifest more easily. With a group that is led with integrity and shared values, you'll find you experience a higher baseline level of peace and energy.

Expanded Group Energy

You do not need a lot of experience in meditation to lead a group or offer a space to sit in silence with others. It is about creating a sacred space for people to come together to practice. While it helps to have experience, it isn't about being an authority, guru, or expert. All you really need is a willing heart to hold a sacred space. Sura Flow meditation is simply the practice of silent sitting.

Group meditation is a service for humanity. Every time a group gets together for the intention of peace, that peace transmits into the rest of the collective experience. It's a sacred service that extends beyond what we can often imagine. Sharing meditation not only affects our personal sense of well-being, but also the well-being of the people around us.

It takes courage to share meditation. It also takes perseverance, humility, and a willingness to show up. Sharing meditation is a true act of service. Like anything worth doing, it means taking a risk — putting yourself out there.

With time you develop confidence leading meditation groups. You and others will still receive a profound benefit. There are many creative ways to offer meditation: at a church, community center, a yoga studio, or even online!

If you'd like extra resources, visit our site where you can learn to lead and offer meditation coaching and programs in a group setting.

If you're interested in hosting your own group, you can play an audio recording provided from *suraflow.org/practices* or use the guided meditation script included at the end of this book.

Sura Flow Meditation Coaching — An Integrated Practice for True Health, Energy and Well-Being

It wasn't until I discovered meditation coaching that I truly discovered my life purpose. While I was teaching yoga and developing my personal executive coaching business, I felt close to my purpose, but it wasn't "it" for me. I still felt like I was missing the mark with what I really wanted to do. Executive coaching was engaging, but it lacked the depth I truly wanted to work with people. It was clear to me yoga could only serve people so far in working with them in their bodies. It was a rewarding job, but I did not feel truly called to become a yoga teacher. It simply wasn't a viable career path for me.

During that time, I was also a Reiki Master and healer, and that felt limited in its own way too. People would come for healing, feel good for that time and a few days afterward, but they weren't taking the steps to heal themselves. What I felt was truly needed was an integrative practice of providing real tools that people could develop on their own — with or without my presence.

The moment I discovered meditation coaching, I knew it was my path. It had what my other roles did not, a way to offer people tools that they could readily use on their own to heal and develop their own self-awareness. Since my clients did not rely on me, it felt naturally more empowering. We could meditate together and raise the energy immediately. In meditation coaching, I began to experience "flow coaching" states where my clients got into a zone of energy where they could effectively hear and coach themselves.

By offering a space of presence and true listening, clients can freely explore, express, and discover the essence of their own truth. With meditation coaching, exchanges became more purposeful. I could be myself. I could go slower, breathe more, and drop in. It was more relaxing. In that space, the people I worked with felt more supported in their own process.

Teaching meditation is deeply fulfilling. I feel it is one of the most resourceful ways to be of service to people. It's also what I enjoy doing the most. It's authentically energetically empowering for clients and myself. When you share this practice with other people, it affirms your own sense of well-being. It also gets you, the practitioner, on the same page as your client.

Meditation is the Future of Coaching

When you deepen your practice, you may naturally develop the inclination to be of service. We are all called to live our purpose. For many of us, that means serving others. You may not know how to do this at first, but your personal practice can be a helpful guide in creating a path of service.

When you are deepening in your own practice, it helps to have a sacred space to explore your experiences and deeper desires. This is where a meditation coach can be instrumental in helping you develop and focus. Imagine extending your practice to another individual. "Meditative coaching" is where you can utilize your own practice to not only raise your own self-awareness, but to cultivate awareness for others.

In meditation coaching, *meditation is the essence of a session.*

Meditation coaching raises energy consciousness. It is centered on the skill of meditation as a way to grow and develop. When presence and energy are cultivated in a session, it allows for natural insight and wisdom to emerge. A mindset of a coach can affect the outcome and flow of a session. When you're in a clear, grounded state, you help cultivate that state together with your client.

Consider meditation coaching as a way to develop your own inner practice. In this approach, you pay close attention to your own internal experience as a coach. You do this as a way to self-regulate and stay balanced, but also provide this space to your client and to intuitively guide the coaching experience.

When you're grounded and centered, it creates a space for your client to fully explore their own inner and outer process. It gives them the energetic freedom to explore and go deeper in the understanding of their own self; their own body awareness, emotions, sensations, thoughts, and realizations. Meditation Coaching is a partnership in raising consciousness.

Framework for Meditation Coaching

The basic structure of a meditation coaching session is the same as the Sura Flow practice. It follows the same basic 3 steps:

1. Relaxation
2. Heart listening
3. Intention

In meditation coaching, you begin with relaxation and presence. You start a session with several minutes of breathing and awareness. This allows you and your client to relax and arrive on the same page. This opens the space for authentic expression, healing, and revelation.

As the coach, you practice heart listening during the session. The core of the session is deep listening while asking powerful coaching questions. You allow the space for unlimited healing and creativity. By slowing down, you create a space for deeper emergence with your client. You can slow down the pace of the session by providing an energy healing or a guided meditation. In these sessions, answers and insights arise spontaneously and with greater ease.

At the end of the session, close quietly with an intention for action. In addition to learning meditation, the client agrees to take positive new actions in their life that lead them toward their desired goals. The end of a session is a good time for a coach to set an intention with the client.

If you decide to take your practice to the next level, this is a sample framework from which a meditation coach works. We offer international training for coaches through our LIBERATE program to people who want to teach meditation.

In the LIBERATE training you learn how to integrate the skills of coaching, energy healing, and meditation. We have found that this process is very effective in raising energy consciousness, for both the client and practitioner.

To learn more about our Certified LIBERATE Meditation Coach training program, visit:
suraflow.org/liberate-meditation-coach-training-course

Meditation Coaching Goes Deeper

When I first started executive coaching, something about the process felt hollow and disconnected. In the beginning, clients would walk through the door and start talking about anything and everything. These were incredibly busy, high-powered executives. They came in with a strong start telling me about their week, unloading much of their stress right into the session. It was a lot of talking and processing which made our time together feel more mental.

Oftentimes, I would feel overwhelmed by the amount of talking and focus on stress during these sessions. I felt like a container for all the random thoughts of my client and sometimes this left me feeling drained. At times, I too, felt very stressed. When my clients talked about high level business strategy, like mergers and acquisitions, I couldn't help but wonder what the deeper source of their stressors were.

Even though I had extensive business experience, I felt I could benefit my clients in a more productive way. I noticed in much of executive coaching that clients seemed more focused on outward goals and achievements, when their core issues were internal.

Their goals became their focus when internally they still felt anxious and stressed. In this case, it wasn't just about what they wanted to achieve, it was how they wanted to live.

> *Meditation coaching focuses on cultivating an inner state that naturally leads to positive, outer results.*

This is when I decided to shift my focus toward serving people through meditation coaching. Mostly because what I experienced as a business and executive coach was a focus on external goals based on egoic tendencies. Our society today is based on results. People are so overly focused on their achievements, they forget about whether what they are doing is actually making themselves and others happy.

Meditation coaching focuses on cultivating an inner state that naturally leads to positive, outer results. When coaching is based only on results, you're moving your client from A to Z without much of a reflective, internal process. Without addressing deeper, core issues such as stress, anxiety, emotions, and deeper desires, a client is likely to experience the same state of being as they did before working with a coach. They may have more money and status, but they might not necessarily have more peace or happiness.

In meditation coaching, we're focused on both the results and the inner experience. We know that it's not just about the end game, but about the journey. To live a life where you feel full of stress and anxiety, while eroding your own health to accumulate external achievements is unwise. If you can live your life in a way where you don't have stress, feel a sense of joy and peace, all while you're achieving your dreams, then that's a fulfilling life worth living.

It wasn't until I focused the process on meditation did I see real, positive, long-lasting results with clients. Teaching them how to slow down, how to breathe and center themselves did wonders. It brought them back to life. I saw them shine with excitement, make big health changes, and reconnect to their loved ones. The results they experienced were profound: they found true inner happiness, purpose, and prosperity.

When we started with silence the noise just fell away. The walls of their defenses came down during meditation. They were less guarded and more authentic. I noticed clients were softer, more connected, and more honest. It was easier to communicate. Instead of feeling overwhelmed by the speed and momentum of a client's thought process, meditation allows for a slower rhythm that opens the space for silence and introspection.

Real results and progress come from a deeper, inner process that includes quiet, reflection, and meditation. They arise from an honest exploration into someone's core beliefs, wounds, and values. Many times it involves identifying and working on constant thought patterns, energy blocks, subconscious and unconscious limiting beliefs that can hold back many areas of life, such as health, love, and relationships.

The practice of meditation coaching provides a gateway to enter a connected, more intuitive process with your client. People know all their own answers. This is what you affirm through meditation coaching. When a person is centered and present, they have greater access to their own wisdom and intuitive insight. A meditation coach provides a space for this access, understanding that the client knows his/her own way.

In sessions, I noticed that when I combined the practice of meditation with coaching, it slowed down the process significantly while adding an element of potency. It was through a slower rhythm that more could be accessed and realized by a client on his/her own. Stillness created a spaciousness the client hadn't experienced before on their own. It is easier to drop into a meditative space when it's facilitated and guided by another, more experienced, practitioner.

When I introduce meditation and energy healing into the process, instead of talking from their headspace, clients connect deeply to themselves and their body. When I ask clients coaching questions in their quiet and mindful state of being, they have more clear, direct access to their own intuitive answers. There's less talking, more direct insight. As a result, there's greater transformation.

This sense of spaciousness also benefits the meditation coach. Not only is it a more relaxing experience, it creates a space of flow and permission for the coach to be inwardly guided. When a coach is in tune and open for anything and everything to flow through higher awareness, it significantly opens the space for potential healing with a client. When both people are grounded and present, it raises the space of consciousness.

Meditation coaching raises the vibration of a session. Sura Flow practice provides a key resource for developing from the inside out. It cultivates self-awareness, emotional awareness, and higher states of being, such as peace and joy. As a meditation coach, you provide a way for people to access calm, while coaching them to realize their deepest intentions. You're creating a sacred space for your clients to gain clarity and focus. It's a vital role that nourishes the coach as much as the client.

When both people are grounded and present, it raises the space of consciousness.

A meditation coach can teach and facilitate meditation, as well as integrate meditation with coaching. This means starting a session with a short guided meditation practice. It only takes a few minutes to reset and return your attention to the center of your being. You'll notice how this facilitation of meditation sets the pace and tone for the rest of your session together.

This simple non-action gives the client an opportunity to practice presence. With breath and body awareness, both the coach and practitioner have a chance to harmonize in a state of calm. In this state, the client moves from the head to the heart through the Sura Flow practice.

Meditation practice helps your client become more embodied and aware. Starting with a few minutes of Sura Flow practice creates a greater sense of clarity and flow throughout the session. Oftentimes there is more ease and less stress, so the session itself becomes less taxing and more rejuvenating.

Develop Your Own Practice Through Meditation Coaching

Meditation coaching has a strong focus on your inner experience as a coach. In this practice, you notice your own breathing, your own sensations, emotions, and body during a session. You remain aware of yourself. You maintain a high level of self-awareness, especially of your energy. This can be different from a regular coaching session where your sense of orientation is primarily focused on your client.

When you lose your inner awareness focus, you can get enveloped into the stories of others. This can drain your own energy and resources. It's like jumping into a raging river with a client without an anchor. Your anchor is your center. Consider it as a grounded anchor for your time with your client so you don't get lost energetically.

Meditation coaching has a strong emphasis on being grounded and centered. It's about energy management. When you're firm in your own energetic space, you can be of greatest service to others. Meditation coaching is a wonderful way to develop yourself, share the practice, and discover a fulfilling vocation. It also meaningfully deepens your own commitment and practice.

An Emerging, High-Growth Market

Stress, anxiety, and depression are currently at all-time highs. People need internal resources now more than ever. According to the World Health Organization, 1 in 13 people suffer from anxiety. In the United States, that's 40 million people, which is 18% of the population, who actually reported having anxiety. In a study conducted by Gallup, it revealed that 55% of Americans are stressed. That's 20% higher than the rest of the world. In a study cited by the American Institute of Stress, 94% of people reported feeling stressed at work.

With the rise of global and political instability, climate change, and uncertainty, people are experiencing tension now more than ever. They are looking for tools to manage their stress and elevate their inner state. People are receptive to new ways to connect spiritually and resource themselves. They want to learn tools on how to develop their inner resilience.

Both coaching and meditation continue to emerge as fast-growing industries. According to the CDC, meditation is one of the fastest-growing health trends. It's currently over a $1 billion dollar market and growing 11% year after year. Consider where yoga was in the early 2000s. Today, it is more widely accepted as a "normal" practice, appealing to both spiritual and secular audiences. More and more people are beginning to explore new forms of spiritual practice that extend beyond traditional religions.

Practices that are secular, inclusive, and universal will take on new meaning during a time we realize how interconnected we truly are. People will seek support in developing their deeper, spiritual selves in a world that becomes inundated by technology, artificial intelligence, and other external threats such as pandemics — massive challenges that are beyond individual control.

As more people develop their yoga practice and extend beyond traditional forms of religion and therapy, the floodgates will open to new ways of healing. Meditation coaching will be the next major mode of healing and development for individual and collective growth. Providing an opportunity to develop one's own resource of calm and centeredness, while ushering others through their own deepest desires and intentions, is the next evolution in coaching.

*Meditation coaching
will be the next
major mode of healing
and development for
individual and
collective growth.*

To receive a free video mini-course on the Sura Flow Meditation Coaching method be sure to visit our website. In this course package, you'll learn how to cultivate your life force energy. You'll receive clarity, focus, and calm to achieve your personal goals. It's an opportunity to deepen your practice through the Sura Flow approach. With your own meditation coaching toolkit, you'll learn essential skills on how to coach yourself and others. Visit: *suraflow.org.*

In Closing

The world is ready for new practices. Integrated practices like Sura Flow provide tools for intuition, empowerment, and true health. This universal, heart-based practice will boost your personal practice and allow you to experience greater ease and flow in your everyday life.

I've included a Sura Flow meditation script for you that you're welcome to practice and share with others in a meditation group experience.

May you receive the true magic of the practice. May these sacred practices lead you to your true self and may you experience true flow.

Love, Sura

Sura Flow Meditation Script

You're welcome to use this script to guide a group medi-tation experience. When you read this meditation guide, remember to center yourself in your heart. Find calm and then read slowly. Take pauses and moments for silence. Connect with yourself and the people around you.

Speak from your heart when you read this meditation script. You can cater the length of time of the meditation to your personal and group needs. You can also record this medita-tion. Kindly be sure to credit suraflow.org. Blessings!

Welcome to Your Sura Flow Meditation

Begin by finding a comfortable, seated position. You're welcome to move and adjust so you feel completely tension-free. Sit straight with your spine tall and relax all the muscles around your midline. You can cross your legs or sit with your feet firmly planted on the floor.

Let's begin by turning your attention inward. Inhale. And exhale, release all the stress and tension from your day. Let your whole body relax.

Bring your attention to your feet. Slowly scan your body, from the bottoms of your feet to the top of your head. Notice if there are any pockets of tension.

(long pause)

Observe yourself sitting. Envision a grounding cord extending from your physical body into the center of the Earth. With your outbreath, imagine any tension, worry, and fear flowing into the Earth from your physical body.

Give yourself full permission to release all thoughts of the past and future. Let go of any thoughts, responsibilities, and feelings of inner tension. With each breath, imagine a gentle wave of relaxation moving through your body.

Gently scan your body again from your feet… all the way through your body… to the top of your head. Let yourself soften from your innermost core.

Now move your attention into your heart. Become aware of inhabiting a compassionate space for yourself.

Inhabit your entire heart space with your attention. Let yourself be relaxed in the center of your heart. Notice the shift as you move your attention from your head into your heart.

Become aware of the shifts that you experience and your sense of awareness and presence.

We'll take three heart breaths.

If you like, you can bring one hand to your heart and one hand to your lower belly. Your hand on your heart allows you to really feel the energy of your heart.

Begin by breathing in through the back of your heart. Gently pause in the center of your heart… (pause) then exhale out through the front of your heart. Pause at the end of your exhale.

Breathe in through the back of your heart, pause… exhale out through the front of your heart. Breathe in calm through the back of your heart, pause… (pause) Breathe out the front of your heart.

Last breath, breathing in through the back of your heart, pause… (pause) Find a moment of stillness… (pause), then breathe out through the front of your heart.

Take three breaths like that on your own. See if you can find a moment of stillness between each in breath and each out breath.

(long pause)

Breathing in peace. Breathing out calm…

Allow your heart center to soften and open.

Let your heart now settle into stillness. Let your heart be still...

You can imagine a candle flame in the center of your heart becoming more and more still, burning brightly.

See if you can envision the radiance of your own heart.

Notice what it's like for your heart space, to be completely still... (pause)

Now let this sense of stillness fill your whole body, your mind, and your energy... Surrender to a complete sense of stillness.

Become aware of the importance of stillness.

From this place of stillness, let yourself feel the presence of your heart.

What is it like to be present in your heart... ?

Breathing in and breathing out. (pause) Taking nice and easy heart breaths. Practicing heart presence.

You can imagine a sphere surrounding your heart representing the energy and intelligence of your own heart.

Notice what it's like to relax into your heart space and to surrender to a sense of stillness.

Notice how calm the body becomes.

Notice how calm your nervous system is.

Let yourself reside in this place of stillness for three more breaths...

Now take this time to be fully aware. Become aware of your feelings, sensations, and thoughts... With the awareness of your heart.

Let yourself listen with heart awareness. Be open to receiving your own insights and impressions. Let yourself open to the natural guidance and energy that flows through you.

(Silence for 5-20 mins)

(You can include the following cues one at a time throughout the time of silence... say simple phrases as gentle reminders: *Be in your heart. Remembering compassion. Listening from your heart. Returning to heart breaths if you need a positive anchor of focus.*)

Let's close this guided meditation by gently focusing on your personal intention.

What is your intention for today? (silence)

Perhaps it's a blessing for humanity, or a healing for yourself.

Let yourself meditate on your intention with love in your heart.

(long pause)

Notice what it's like to meditate on your heartfelt intention. (silence for 2-3 mins)

Now take this time to surrender fully, both your intention and your practice. Let's take a moment to express gratitude for this practice.

Now we will close and complete today's meditation. Gather up your energy and ground it again down to the Earth. Bring your hands together in prayer.

Blessings and namaste. (bow)

About the Author

Sura is a highly experienced Meditation Coach and Trainer, who is passionate about helping people heal through the practice of meditation. She is the founder of the Sura Flow Meditation Coaching method which has been taught to thousands of students all around the world.

Sura first discovered meditation while working a high-stress life on Wall Street. After receiving profound healing benefits from her personal practice, she left corporate life in New York to study meditation in the countryside of Asia. Through years of practice, she developed her signature approach to meditation: a softer, effortless practice called Sura Flow. This simple 3-step, heart-centered approach cultivates energy flow, creativity, and inner guidance for self-actualization.

With extensive experience in both the spiritual and business world, she currently offers Certified Meditation and Leadership programs based on her unique 3-step approach. Sura currently lives in Hawaii where she devotes her time to teaching and creative meditation.

You can learn more about Sura at **suraflow.org**.

Made in the USA
Monee, IL
22 January 2021